CW01371831

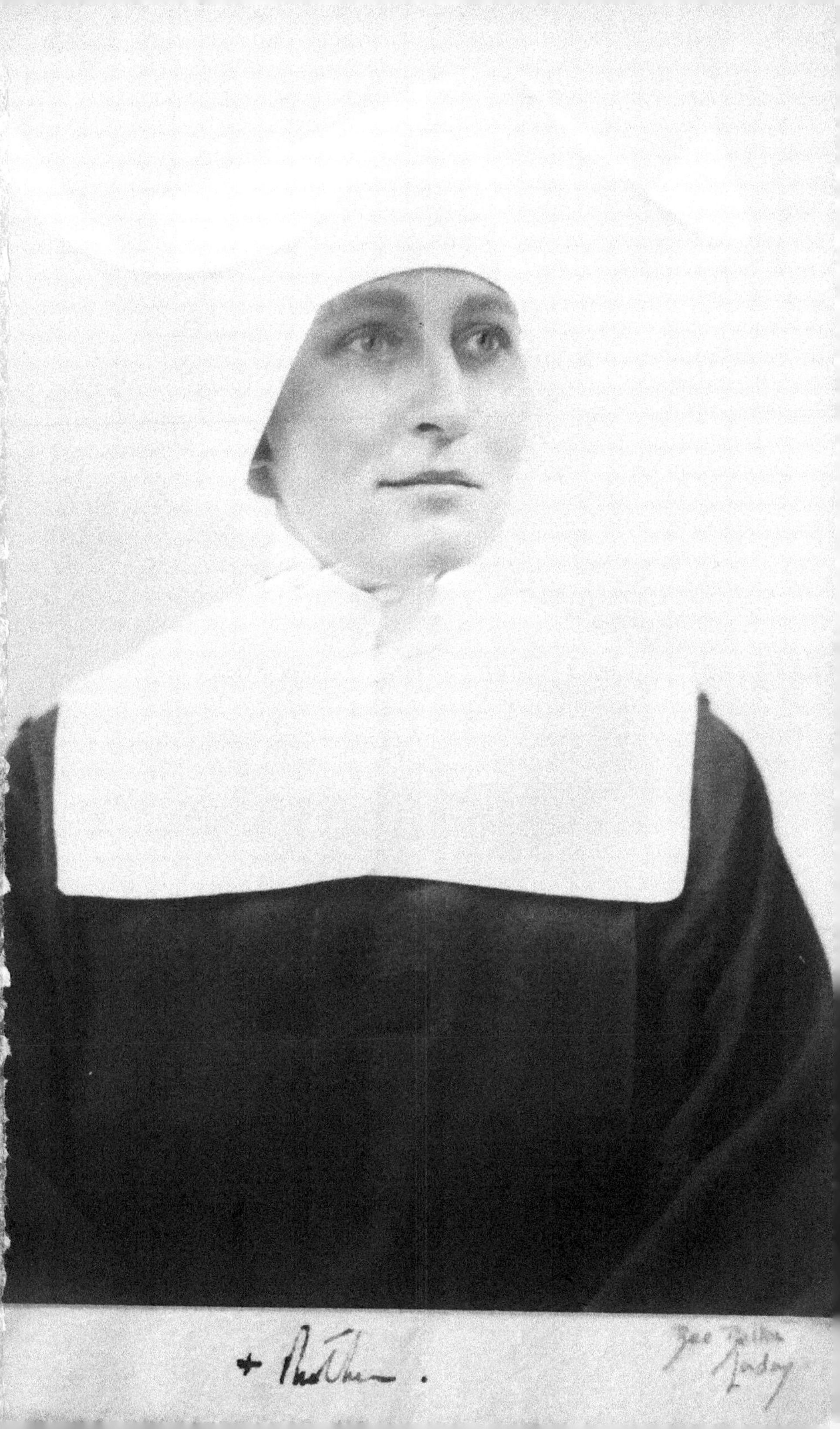

Mother of Invention

*Mother Teresa and the
Franciscan Servants of Jesus and Mary*

— BRIDGET GILLARD —

Sacristy Press

Sacristy Press
PO Box 612, Durham, DH1 9HT

www.sacristy.co.uk

First published in 2025 by Sacristy Press, Durham

Copyright © Bridget Gillard 2025
The moral rights of the author have been asserted.

All rights reserved, no part of this publication may be reproduced or transmitted in any form or by any means, electronic, mechanical photocopying, documentary, film or in any other format without prior written permission of the publisher.

Every reasonable effort has been made to trace the copyright holders of material reproduced in this book, but if any have been inadvertently overlooked the publisher would be glad to hear from them.

Sacristy Limited, registered in England & Wales, number 7565667

British Library Cataloguing-in-Publication Data
A catalogue record for the book is available from the British Library

ISBN 978-1-78959-373-0

To
Mother Mary Agnes

And in memory of
Mother Teresa
Mother Hilary
Sister Giovanna
Sister Margaret
Sister Bernadine
Sister Faith
Sister Mary
Sister Mary Bride
Sister Elizabeth

Contents

Illustrations vi
Foreword ix
Preface...xii
Acknowledgements...xiv

Part 1 1
Chapter 1. An inauspicious start...................................... 3
Chapter 2. An American adventure 12
Chapter 3. War and pacifism 18
Chapter 4. Four years at St Hilary................................... 28
Chapter 5. Blisland—"This holy and peaceful place"................ 41
Chapter 6. A pattern of living in Paisley 47
Chapter 7. A pair of odd adventurers............................. 56
Chapter 8. The road to London................................. 69
Chapter 9. An island interlude.................................. 82

Part 2 91
Chapter 10. "Not imposbury but very difficult" 93
Chapter 11. Posbury St Francis: Prayer and work................. 101
Chapter 12. Post-war growth....................................114
Chapter 13. A change of rule 127
Chapter 14. End of an era.......................................142
Chapter 15. Unsustainable loss 149
Chapter 16. Sister Death 159

Epilogue 170
Afterword 173

Appendix 1. Members of the Franciscan Servants of Jesus and
Mary in life vows... 177
Appendix 2. The Constitution, Statutes and Rules of the
Franciscan Servants of Jesus and Mary........................... 180

Index 188

Illustrations

Front cover: Portrait of Mother Teresa, founder of the FSJM. The painting occupied a prominent position at the top of the main staircase at Posbury. Reproduced by kind permission of the PSFT.

Frontispiece: Studio portrait of Mother Teresa taken in the early 1930s after the Community had moved to London. Reproduced by kind permission of the PSFT.

1. Grace Costin on the beat as Oxford's first policewoman in 1917. Reproduced by kind permission of Michael Burgess.
2. Grace in the early 1920s holding a baby with her friend, mentor and sometime sparring partner Bernard Walke and his wife Annie to her left. Reproduced by kind permission of Michael Burgess.
3. Procession following the blessing of the FSJM's house in Oakley Crescent, London in 1933. Bishop Curzon can be seen emerging from the house preceded by, from left to right, Sister Margaret, Mother Teresa and Sister Bernadine. Reproduced by kind permission of the PSFT.
4. St Francis House, the home of the FSJM in Whitwell, Isle of Wight. The importance of nature to the Community is evidenced by the open windows and well-tended garden. Reproduced by kind permission of the PSFT.
5. From left to right Sister Bernadine, Mother Teresa and Sister Margaret outside St Francis House. Behind them is the banner first used on their missions in southeast Cornwall. The photograph was possibly taken on the occasion of the blessing of the house by the Bishop of Portsmouth in May 1938. Reproduced by kind permission of the PSFT.

ILLUSTRATIONS vii

6. The main house at Posbury with its thatch prior to the reroofing in slate in 1963. In front of the chapel to the left is Sister Mary's greenhouse and her well-established herbaceous border can be seen on the right. Reproduced with kind permission from the collection of Mr Phillips.
7. The chapel at Posbury converted from a former stable block. The door leads into the main body of the chapel, the half dormer window lights the priest's bedroom above the sacristy and to its right lies the priest's sitting room. Reproduced by kind permission of the PSFT.
8. Photograph marking the clothing of Sister Mary and Sister Bride on 26 April 1946. Sister Mary, to the left of Mother Teresa and Sister Bride to her right wear the round collar of a novice. Seated on the ground are Sister Bernadine and Sister Hilary to the right. Reproduced by kind permission of the PSFT.
9. Sister Hilary, departing in some style for her pilgrimage to Assisi in 1951, being bid farewell by Sister Mary. Reproduced by kind permission of the PSFT.
10. Sister Agnes outside the front door at Posbury on the day she made her life vows, 1 July 1969. Reproduced by kind permission of Mother Mary Agnes.
11. Mother Hilary and Sister Faith on the front lawn at Posbury with their dog Leo in the 1970s. On the hillside in the distance is Posbury Clump bought by the sisters to save the trees from being felled. Reproduced by kind permission of the PSFT.
12. Group photo of the sisters outside the backdoor at Posbury in the late 1980s. From left to right Sister Bride, Sister Elizabeth, Mother Hilary, Sister Mary, Sister Faith and Sister Giovanna—seated with their dog Max. Sisters Bride, Mary and Giovanna are wearing their gardening clothes. Reproduced by kind permission of the PSFT.
13. Sister Mary seated on her tractor with Mother Hilary holding Max, and Sister Giovanna. They are accompanied by Extern Sister Molly Boxall, who lived nearby and nursed Mother Teresa while she was dying. Photo: © Chris Chapman.

14. Mother Hilary seated in the kitchen at Posbury with from left to right Sisters Bride, Elizabeth and Mary. Behind them was the habitually running aga which made the room one of the most welcoming in the house. The jug on the table and poster on the wall are souvenirs from their pilgrimages to Assisi. Photo: © Chris Chapman.
15. The garden altar rescued from the graveyard at St Hilary in 1953 with a surround built by the sisters from blocks of red sandstone brought from Posbury Clump. The reproduction della Robbia plaque was brought back from a pilgrimage to Italy. Reproduced by kind permission of the PSFT.
16. Mother Hilary poses with the broadcaster Sir Harry Secombe, Sister Mary and Sister Giovanna after he visited the FSJM in the 1980s. Reproduced by kind permission of the PSFT.
17. Service of Benediction at the garden altar at the conclusion of an Open Day - the juxtaposition of High Anglican practice, natural setting and family atmosphere typical of the FSJM. Reproduced by kind permission of the PSFT.
18. Photograph of Sister Giovanna and Mother Hilary from the exhibition *A Positive View of the Third Age*. Photo: © Chris Chapman.

Back Cover: Photograph of a cell before the house was cleared prior to sale. © Chris Chapman.

Foreword

Taken to Posbury St Francis when I was about two years old is at least an indication of a lifetime's experience of the community. From my boyhood, I remember a small, round and light-hearted lady dressed in brown, with a large red cross emblazoned on her habit and a huge brown hat shaped like a snow shovel over her head. This was my father's sister, who made her annual holiday in Paisley with my parents, a town where she and my father had grown up. She had one of those West of Scotland accents that had crisp, clear consonants that created a staccato effect when she spoke. For the rest of her life, I was to know her as Aunt Betty. Her "religious" name was Sister Elizabeth, named after the Franciscan saint, Elizabeth of Hungary. For me, she remains an "incognito" saint. That incognito element in the Sisters is the one that Bridget Gillard reveals in this book.

When I visited Posbury after I was ordained, it didn't take long to realize that the older Sisters, although holding the ordained in high esteem, were equally critical of what we lacked, which made conversations at Posbury somewhat nerve-racking. They expected the highest of standards from clergy and told us so. Criticism was not only reserved for clergy, but also for much of the Anglican Church, which for them didn't adhere adequately to the disciplines and insights of Anglo-Catholicism.

When my aunt died, I asked Mother Hilary if I might hold on to Aunt Betty's Daily Office books, which had been for her a lifetime's "vade mecum"; books that contained all the hymns, psalms, readings and prayers for the various praying periods for each day. In between many of the pages were dog-eared prayer cards, which my aunt had collected. I longed to preserve these and whatever Aunt Betty left behind, including a ballpoint Bic pen in her habit pocket. That was all. "No", I was immediately informed, I could not have her office books nor the pen for the simple reason that they were the possessions of the Franciscan Servants of Jesus and Mary and were made available only for their use. Such blunt but undemonstrative abandonment of the trappings of possession, in the lives of the Sisters, coupled with a guileless obedience to the superiors of the community, as Bridget Gillard points out, were to be found throughout the small community. Of course, there were notable moments of friction and testing, which are at the heart of any religious community.

There were attempts made in the community's earlier days in Posbury, by a larger Anglican religious order, to incorporate Posbury St Francis. That idea was given short shrift, which was for me indicative of a determination to live and indeed to die as a small praying and servant community given to care for the earth and its creatures and, while they were able, to demonstrate that style of Franciscan life when they took part in missions. Bridget Gillard's book constantly portrays this confident determination in Mother Teresa, the founder, and consequently the Sisters who joined her.

This book breaks open the beginnings, the inspirations and life of a community that have been in danger of slipping out of memory and so out of history. When it comes to the point that the remaining Sister "welcomes Sister Death", as Francis himself would have put it, this book will secure the story, the gift, the love and discipline and the Sisters' equally simple trust in God. The Franciscan Servants of Jesus and Mary, as a community, has in one sense come to an end, but the vision of the community lives on in the Posbury St Francis Trust, which advocates and indeed makes available support for ventures such as spiritual direction training and retreats. Bridget Gillard, in her writing, gives depth and energy to a story that enables a continuum of the Sisters' dynamic.

Mother Teresa was indeed a formidable lady, but when she counselled individual Sisters and recalcitrant priests, such as me, there was always tenderness there at the roots of her demanding expectations. Not much room was given to idle chatter or gossip, despite the occasional slippage.

This Franciscan "spirit" in the Posbury Sisters, Bridget Gillard has exposed with a gentleness and insight that can, if we have a mind and heart to be open enough, inspire today, in a world that is desperate for indications of holiness. That holiness is seldom found in large displays and publicity, but in the small, almost the hidden. In St John's Gospel, Nathanael, when Jesus of Nazareth is pointed out to him, questions: "Can anything good come out of Nazareth?" I can only match that with "Can anything good come out of Posbury St Francis?" With Bridget Gillard's help, the answer to that is "yes", but only if this story is read and heard as a source for new inspiration.

Martin Shaw
Assistant Bishop of the Diocese of Exeter
May 2024

Preface

This is the story of how a woman, the daughter of a bigamous marriage, with no money, connections or academic background, founded her own religious order which, at its height, was visited by over 2,000 people a year.

There is nothing conventional about the life and religious journey of Grace Costin. After a family tragedy caused her to reject God, she began on the long path back to faith through pioneering social work, a solo journey across the United States and a brief interlude as one of the first women police officers. There followed a fleeting ministry as Sister Teresa in the Order of St Anne, before she abandoned the confines of an enclosed order to join a progressive project rehabilitating young women offenders. This brought her into contact with the charismatic priest Bernard Walke, with whom she formed a loving but combative working partnership before experiencing a calling to create a religious order unlike any that had existed before. Her quest took her from remote parishes in Cornwall to the slums of Paisley, an inner-city parish in 1930s London, and the Isle of Wight, until finally she found what she was searching for in the personal ads of the *Daily Telegraph*—a "Typical Thatched Devon farmhouse".

And so, in the middle of the Second World War, aged 54, with a heart condition and no money, she set out to transform the run-down house in a remote corner of Devon into the community she had dreamed of for so long. With the help of a series of remarkable women she had attracted along the way, she created Posbury St Francis—a community, not a convent, with Sisters, not nuns, and a Mother, but not a Mother Superior.

This book draws on Teresa's own candid, hand-written memoir, the transcript of an interview she gave when she turned 90 and the many hundreds of newsletters she wrote to those who supported her project at Posbury. Here she shared her radical beliefs in pacifism, ecology, anti-materialism, human rights, race equality and social justice. All direct quotes from Mother Teresa and her successor, Mother Hilary, come from these sources.

The Sisters were highly sociable and the number of their friends and associates was great. To avoid confusion, I have generally limited the people named to those referred to in Teresa's writings and the *Newsletter*s. As a consequence, there will be many individuals, including those who went to Posbury to test their vocations, who were of great importance to the Sisters but remain unnamed. I hope the general references to Sisters, Externs, friends and neighbours in some way acknowledge their importance to the FSJM.

This book is a simple narrative, and no attempt is made to provide a theological context for the order.

Bridget Gillard
Exe Valley
Summer 2024

Acknowledgements

In addition to learning about the extraordinary life of Mother Teresa, one of the great joys of writing this book has been getting to know Mother Mary Agnes. She has been immensely generous with her time, sharing her memories and insights into the FSJM and her comments on my book have been invaluable—without her contributions it would be much diminished. I am also most grateful to Sister Giovanna, who gave so much of her time when I first started researching the book. She shared a wealth of information and, along with her friend and helper, Lin Denner, kindly sought out sources of information including the recording of *Through the Garden Gate*, which we watched together at The Tractor Shed, with Sister happily reliving the whole experience.

Bishop Martin Shaw has been a source of great encouragement from the very first, giving me access to the FSJM archive and sharing his, sometimes very funny, memories of the Sisters, especially his beloved Aunty Betty (Sister Elizabeth).

After I began my research, the Posbury St Francis Trust was formed, ably led by the Venerable Trevor Jones, who very kindly asked me to join as a trustee. I would like to thank all my fellow trustees for their great support and encouragement of my work.

I am very grateful to Father Roddy Leece, who recommended I publish an article about my book to drum up interest. This proved to be excellent advice, and on Trevor Jones' suggestion I contacted the *Church Times*, who published my article in September 2022. I would like to thank Vicky Walker at the *Church Times* for her support and for the inspired title "Mother of Invention".

The publication of the article attracted some excellent new sources of information, including the transcript of Mother Teresa's interview with Canon Leslie Rule Wilson. This was sent to me, along with a photograph of Grace as a policewoman, by Canon Rule's friend Canon Michael

Burgess. I am so grateful to Canon Burgess for getting in contact and for all the other helpful information he provided. The article also brought me into contact with Michael Blain, who, as a student at Mirfield, went to Posbury several times to visit his former vicar Father Cecil Gault and had many recollections of the Sisters and Mother Hilary. The *Church Times* article was also read by Michael Lowe, one of the original members of the West Midlands working party, and I am very grateful to him for sharing his memories.

Thank you to both Father John Fairweather and June Roberts, who both gave valuable insights into experiencing Posbury as an ordinand and as an Extern respectively. June also explained the governance of the order in the difficult years after Mother Hilary was diagnosed with dementia.

I am very grateful to my mother, Ruth Richards, for sharing her many memories of Posbury, the Sisters and Father Hooper, for answering countless questions and for access to her extensive back catalogue of *Crockfords*!

This book is greatly enhanced by the addition of some beautiful photographs taken by Chris Chapman. Chris has been really encouraging of the project from the outset and we spent a memorable day photographing the house and grounds before they were put up for sale. My photos proved a useful aide memoire, whereas his are elegiac works of art.

This book owes a very great deal to my friend Peter Beacham. Peter is a lyrical writer on Devon, an historic buildings expert, the author of the current "Pevsner" for Cornwall and a self-supporting minister whose association with Posbury goes back to the 1970s, when he attended his ordination retreat there. I could not have had anyone better qualified to read through my book chapter by chapter, offering wonderful advice and encouragement.

I am also very grateful to John Scott for sharing the extract about Posbury from his father's memoir.

I had a lovely weekend in Porthcurno, where I was privileged to meet Bridget Hugh-Jones and Bobbie Thomas, who both shared their memories of the Sisters when they came to stay at The Haven.

I am very grateful to Sacristy Press for publishing the book and in particular to Natalie Watson for all her help and guidance.

Finally, I would like to thank my husband Ian and my son Guy, who have patiently listened to five years of Posbury talk.

Figure 1: Grace Costin on the beat as Oxford's first policewoman in 1917.

Figure 2: Grace in the early 1920s holding a baby with her friend, mentor and sometime sparring partner Bernard Walke and his wife Annie to her left.

Figure 3: Procession following the blessing of the FSJM's house in Oakley Crescent, London in 1933. Bishop Curzon can be seen emerging from the house preceded by, from left to right, Sister Margaret, Mother Teresa and Sister Bernadine.

Figure 4: St Francis House, the home of the FSJM in Whitwell, Isle of Wight. The importance of nature to the Community is evidenced by the open windows and well-tended garden.

Figure 5: From left to right Sister Bernadine, Mother Teresa and Sister Margaret outside St Francis House. Behind them is the banner first used on their missions in southeast Cornwall. The photograph was possibly taken on the occasion of the blessing of the house by the Bishop of Portsmouth in May 1938.

Part 1

CHAPTER 1

An inauspicious start

It began badly. The circumstances of Grace Costin's early life were inauspicious, as not infrequently seems to be true of many later called to the life of the religious. She was born in Folkestone on 27 October 1888 to Thomas and Annie Costin. Her father was a bricklayer and home was a small cottage in a row abutting the South Eastern Main Line on the edge of the expanding town. She was baptized at two months at Christ Church, Folkestone, and for a time the young couple and their daughter lived a life that was poor but seemingly respectable. However, before Grace was three years old, Annie discovered her marriage to Thomas was bigamous and her daughter illegitimate. In great distress, she left her "husband" and fled with Grace to live with her widowed father, Edward Dawson, in Hastings. The circumstances of her devastating discovery are not known.*

By the time of the 1891 census, Annie, her father Edward and Grace were living at 44 Baybrook Road in a row of tall terraced houses behind Hastings station. Annie is described in the census as the head of the house who let apartments, but neither she nor her father (a gardener) were listed as working at this time. Annie then met and married a widower, William Parsons, whose first wife had tragically died at the age of 22, leaving a two-year-old daughter, Ellen. William, a general labourer,

---

* Years later, when recalling the events as a 90-year-old woman, Mother Teresa described a more romantic version of events, as told to her by her mother, who no doubt wished to make the story of her early years less pathetic. Grace was led to believe her mother, the daughter of a farmer, had married an aristocratic ne'er-do-well only to later find out he was married to someone else. This information was given to Canon L Rule Wilson in a recorded interview with Mother Hilary in 1978.

3

although relatively poorly paid, would have brought respectability for Annie and her daughter.

Grace was six when her mother remarried, and William's daughter Ellen was three. It seems likely Annie, whom Grace described as having a child-like gaiety and simplicity, would have been a loving stepmother to Ellen. The relationship between Grace and her stepfather, however, was more problematic. William was pathologically jealous of her and would frequently warn Annie: "That girl of yours, she'll turn out exactly like her father."

William and Annie went on to have a number of other children together, including a boy who suffered from tuberculosis. Annie was anxious that the children should receive a good education and Grace and her siblings were sent to a church school, which charged modest fees, rather than the free local board school. By the time she was 15, however, Grace had to leave in order to help her mother with the housework and nurse her sick half-brother. She was immensely fond of all her siblings, while at the same time conscious she was very different to them in her thoughts and ambitions.

Nursing her brother through his final illness brought them even closer, but the experience had a profound effect on Grace, who at the age of 16 was still only a child herself. She had been brought up to believe everything that happened in life was God's will, and so prayed fervently throughout her sibling's illness that he would get better. Then, when informed by her mother that he was dying, she prayed equally fervently that he should not suffer at the end. After he died in great pain, the distraught young woman vowed to God in front of his coffin, "I believe in you, but I want nothing more to do with you. If this is what you are like, I'm finished."

After this traumatic episode, Grace's own health broke down. She suffered heart problems, culminating, when she was 17, in major surgery followed by a three-month stay in hospital. On finally being discharged, her one desire was to find a job which would keep her out of the house. Her relationship with her stepfather had not improved over the years and his constant verbal attacks undermined any attempts by Annie to create a happy home atmosphere. Mindful of her physical limitations post-surgery, Grace decided to answer an advertisement for a lady receptionist at a photographer's studio on the seafront at St Leonards-on-Sea, a popular tourist destination not far from the family home. Her mother was horrified at the prospect of her young daughter spending time alone with the unknown male photographer, but after meeting Grace's prospective employer, Annie felt satisfied he was a gentleman and posed no threat to her daughter.

All went well at first, with Grace particularly enjoying the wet days when no one came into the studio. Then she could read for hours on end without interruption. Unfortunately, her mother's faith in a gentlemanly code of conduct was to prove misplaced. Grace's striking good looks—a curvaceous figure, thick brown, wavy hair, deep-set blue eyes and a beautifully defined mouth—were not lost on the photographer. One day in the darkroom he could not resist making a pass, to which Grace responded with a well-aimed punch. Such was her desire to be out of the house, she determined not to tell her mother about the incident and continued at the photographic studio for the rest of the summer. As autumn approached and her health improved, she felt strong enough to plan moving away from home permanently and decided to look for situations as a mother's help—a position for which she was already experienced and which would allow her to "live in".

Against Annie's wishes she took a situation with a family in London, insisting life would be better for everyone if she and her stepfather were no longer under the same roof. She moved into a pleasant small house in Acton with the Rowden family to help with their three young children. For three years, she was happy in her work, until Mrs Rowden had a fourth child. Mr Rowden, whose behaviour had until this point been entirely correct, suddenly began to stare at her strangely and generally behave in a way which made her feel uncomfortable. One evening he came into her room on the pretext of delivering a letter which had arrived by the last post and made his real intentions clear: "My dear girl, you'll never escape; if it isn't me, it will be someone else." Grace, trembling with fear and rage, threatened to scream if he touched her. Following the incident, she made arrangements to leave as soon as she could.

She was forced to take the next situation which came along, and when this did not work out, found herself cheap lodgings in Fulham with a pair of attractive young sisters. While Grace was undoubtedly brave and resourceful, she was still only 20 years old and relatively naive. After describing to a male friend the curious comings and goings of her flatmates at night, he pointed out exactly what it was they did for a living and the necessity for her to find somewhere else to live as soon as possible.

At this point, she felt her health had recovered sufficiently for her to train as a nurse—a career she had been considering for a while. She successfully applied for a probationer post advertised in the *Nursing Mirror* and in spring 1909 began work in a very fashionable nursing home in Chelsea. Most of the patients were aristocratic men, and Grace later recalled the work as interesting but revelatory of "various odd aspects of life". Her recent experiences had made her more worldly-wise and, when she learnt the matron had a policy of only taking on good-looking nurses, she began to look for work elsewhere.

She later described herself during these first years away from home as "a flippant young woman" who lived a "wild and pagan" life. Nevertheless, underneath this superficial frivolity she had begun to develop an increasing sense of social injustice. She later recalled: "All my interest and compassion was with those who rebelled against and broke the law, and those whose circumstances gave no opportunity for a right manner of life which could also be a happy and satisfying one."

Grace finally went home in 1909 to spend the Easter holiday in Hastings. Driven by an impulse she could not explain, she attended the Holy Week nightly services at Christ Church, St Leonards. These were conducted by Father Andrew, a visiting friar from the Community of St John the Divine, who staffed the mission church of St Philip, Plaistow. Grace had never attended an Anglo-Catholic church before and was struck by the magnificence of the church interior with its soaring arches, jewel-like stained glass and profusion of carved and painted decoration. Despite the beauty of her surroundings, she recalled "sleepwalking" through the liturgy, until Maundy Thursday when she suddenly felt compelled to ask Father Andrew to hear her confession. Looking back on the event, she attributed this uncharacteristic action to "the inner determined effort of my soul, to disentangle itself from all that was hindering her access to God". Making her confession was a transformative experience which she later described as a "conversion" which "brought great changes into my exterior life".

The man who inspired this radical change of heart, Father Andrew, was the son of a colonel, who, as an undergraduate at Oxford, had volunteered at a mission house in the heart of the deprived East End of London.[1] Moved by the work there, he went on to co-found his own religious order.[2] A portrait of Father Andrew, made around the time he met Grace, shows a man with powerful features whose deep-set hooded eyes and slightly weary air are countered by a penetrating gaze.[3] Despite their contrasting backgrounds, Grace recognized in Father Andrew someone who responded to the poor and disadvantaged with a compassion and understanding similar to her own.

Father Andrew was anxious to assist Grace but recognized that her antipathy towards her stepfather William had the potential to impair her journey back to Christian life. He refused to give her absolution until she promised to forgive him. There then followed an impasse with Grace arguing that Father Andrew had no idea how badly her stepfather had behaved towards her. This was resolved by Grace eventually promising to try to forgive William, to which Father Andrew responded, "That will do, as anything you promise to do, you'll do."

Shortly afterwards Grace left the Chelsea nursing home to begin her general training at the Royal Sea Bathing Hospital at Margate. Unfortunately, the combination of an unsympathetic matron and the arduousness of the work proved too much for her precarious health. At this point, Father Andrew, who had become her confidant as well as her spiritual director, found her a post at the Royal Surrey County Hospital. She managed to complete two and a half more years of training before in 1911 suffering a further heart episode which required major surgery. At this point, her doctor advised that continuing her training would put her health at considerable risk and consequently she was forced to abandon nursing for good.

What her next move should be was by no means obvious. Following the profound experience of her conversion and her continuing relationship with Father Andrew, she began to consider whether she had a religious vocation but felt no attraction to the conventional life of a nun. She was still working on forgiving her stepfather, but the idea of returning to live at home was out of the question. After taking a series of uninspiring jobs in social work, she came into contact with a woman who was to play a key role in her development.

Lady Henry Somerset was a high-profile member of the Women's Temperance Movement and was well known throughout Britain and North America for her powerful fundraising speeches and philanthropic work. She believed in a hands-on approach, spending part of her time at the White Ribbon Settlement House in Bow, where cheap, nourishing food and medical care were provided for children in need.[4] When Lady Henry and Grace's paths crossed in late 1913, she invited Grace to join another of her projects, a pioneering colony for women inebriates at Duxhurst in Surrey.

Duxhurst was a remarkable place; a community of purpose-built, half-timbered, thatched cottages built around a village green presenting an idyllic version of country life. These simple, attractive cottages housed working-class women, while nearby Hope House provided accommodation for middle-class women who could afford to pay for their treatment, and a converted manor house afforded a refuge for society ladies and the occasional celebrity.[5] There was much about Duxhurst that was innovative, including the focus on rehabilitation, the lack of restraints (residents could come and go as they wished) and the non-judgemental atmosphere. The latter would have been particularly attractive to Grace. Here was a community run almost entirely by women, where women worked together to support themselves and their children, albeit with tasks and accommodation apportioned according to their class. They were practically self-sufficient: growing fruit and vegetables; keeping cows, bees, chickens and pigs and learning various crafts including basketwork, weaving and pottery.[6]

Grace's admiration for Lady Henry was undoubted. She described her as "the first person to try and reform inebriate girls and women without harsh treatment and repressive methods". But it was another woman living in the colony at Duxhurst who was to have the more profound effect on the 25-year-old woman. Although non-denominational, at the heart of Duxhurst stood the church of St Mary and the Angels whose vernacular exterior hid a highly decorated Anglo-Catholic tabernacle, fitted out with silverware and works of art, provided by its aristocratic patron.[7] Lady Henry's support for Anglo-Catholicism at Duxhurst did not end with the church building—in a small purpose-built house lived two women in their early 50s, Sister Ivy and Sister Rosanna, who were practising anchoresses.* Grace was drawn to Sister Ivy, who she referred to as Mother. Doubtless she was seeking a maternal influence after having to leave her own unhappy home. Superficially, Lady Henry represented those qualities Grace most admired and was by all accounts a truly inspirational and charismatic figure. Nevertheless, it was to the woman who had withdrawn from the secular world and its concerns that she felt most drawn. Through Mother Ivy she began to explore the Christian faith further and to discuss what it meant to lead the life of a professing Christian.

Life at Duxhurst would have presented a welcome contrast to Grace's previous unsatisfactory experiences of social work. However, this seemingly idyllic female Utopia had a curiously unsettling effect on the young woman, which even her burgeoning relationship with Mother Ivy and the satisfaction she gained from their theological discussions could not dispel. Lady Henry sensed Grace's restlessness, advising she was too young to settle for life in the colony and should see more of the world in order to determine where her true vocation lay.

What was the cause of Grace's unease? There is no mention of thwarted romantic relationships or a desire for a family of her own in any of her writings. By the time she reached Duxhurst, she was already past the age when many women would have married—her mother, Annie, had made her first disastrous "marriage" at the age of 22 and Lady Henry was just 20 when she married. Lady Henry's marriage, although legally legitimate, proved to be as scandalous and unhappy as that of poor Annie. She had made a seemingly good match to the second son of the Duke of Beaufort, but just six years later took the highly unusual step of seeking a divorce. She had discovered her husband was homosexual and successfully sued for the custody of their son. Perhaps these painful experiences, alongside the many sad stories of the women seeking refuge at Duxhurst and her

---

* An anchoress is a female anchorite—someone who has chosen to withdraw from society and live a life of prayer. As part of their religious observance, they take a vow of stability of place, meaning they will not leave their building (often a cell attached to a church) unless to attend church.

own experiences of assault, had put Grace off the idea of matrimony permanently.

As poor health had frustrated her attempts to acquire a nursing qualification, she needed to find some other way to earn a living while staying true to her social conscience. The intensity of her relationship with Mother Ivy suggests she was taking her religious life increasingly seriously, but this was tempered by a growing desire to broaden her horizons. Her unwillingness to settle down seems unremarkable in the modern world where gap years and travelling for self-discovery are commonplace. In the early years of the twentieth century, however, travel was only for the very rich seeking cultural diversion or the less privileged seeking work. Lady Henry, observing the restiveness of her young friend and perhaps feeling a degree of empathy with the young woman due to her difficult family background, decided to assist in her search for new experiences.

It was Lady Henry's suggestion that Grace should go to America. As president of the British Women's Temperance Association, she had frequently travelled to the United States promoting the organization and had formed numerous connections there. She had recently heard from her sister Adeline, the Duchess of Bedford, about the work of a newly founded religious community, the Order of St Anne in Boston, which had a particular interest in the care of children.[8] It was arranged that Grace would stay with the Sisters of St Anne until she could find suitable work. Lady Henry had frequently arranged and paid for the passage of women and children who wished to emigrate to America and Canada following stays at Duxhurst,[9] and happily did the same for Grace.

And so it was that on 9 May 1914 Grace set sail from Liverpool, her benefactress having ensured she travelled in the comfort of second class rather than steerage. Back at Duxhurst, Mother Ivy and Lady Henry must have felt reassured that while their protégé would be gaining the new experiences she craved, she would be safely chaperoned by the Sisters of St Anne. However, a meeting with a fellow passenger on the voyage out was to plant another idea into Grace's restless mind.

Notes

[1] "Andrew (Society of the Divine Compassion)", Wikipedia (last modified 29 April 2022), <https://en.wikipedia.org/wiki/Andrew_(Society_of_the_Divine_Compassion)>, accessed 17 May 2024.

[2] The Advisory Council on Religious Communities, *Guide to the Religious Communities of the Anglican Communion* (London: A. R. Mowbray & Co., 1951), p. 2.

[3] Father Andrew, Society of the Divine Compassion, "A Portrait by Claude Harris. Father Andrew in his forties", Facebook post, 31 March 2019, <https://www.facebook.com/FatherAndrewSDC>, accessed 17 May 2024.

[4] R. Black, *A Talent for Humanity: The life and work of Lady Henry Somerset* (Chippenham: Anthony Rowe Publishing, 2010), p. 94.

[5] Black, *A Talent for Humanity*, p. 74.

[6] Black, *A Talent for Humanity*, p. 79.

[7] Black, *A Talent for Humanity*, p. 76.

[8] Black, *A Talent for Humanity*, p. 106.

[9] Black, *A Talent for Humanity*, p. 84.

CHAPTER 2

An American adventure

The second-class accommodation on board the SS *Arabic* was less than a quarter full when Grace embarked on her voyage to America. Almost half the passengers were, like her, unaccompanied women and among the ladies' maids and the wives travelling to join their husbands was a 30-year-old widow of Dutch and Russian descent, Mrs Hardy, and her two young daughters. Grace struck up a friendship with Mrs Hardy and learnt she was going to Missouri, where she had secured a post as a Travellers' Aid agent at the recently built Kansas City Union Station. Mrs Hardy, observing how well Grace got on with her elder daughter and no doubt feeling rather daunted at the prospect of living and working in a new country, suggested Grace should come and stay with them. Grace, however, with only the five pounds required to land in the United States in her pocket and the guarantee of accommodation at the convent in Boston, did not feel able to accept her offer.

Instead, she went ahead with her plan to stay with the Sisters at St Anne's House, a tall red-brick building situated in the leafy Beacon Hill area of Boston. The convent had been created just three years earlier by a group of four women who, seeking to form a community, had renovated a former clergy house of the Community of St John the Evangelist (the Cowley Fathers), which had been allowed to fall into disrepair by a previous tenant.* One of the Cowley Fathers, Frederick Cecil Powell, had in 1910 founded the Order of St Anne in Arlington Heights, Massachusetts and accepted the new community in Beacon Hill as a branch of this new order in 1912.[1]

---

* The Sisters remained at 44 Temple Street until the building was demolished in 1953 after being condemned. It is now a public garden.

When Father Powell agreed that Grace could come and board with the Sisters while she looked for work, he no doubt hoped she might eventually decide to join the order. It did not take long for her to realize his intentions and, while appreciating his interest and kindness, she felt increasingly under pressure to pursue a vocation she sensed she did not have. She would not have realized it at the time, but the ensuing battle of wills with a member of the clergy was to become a recurring theme in her life. Grace stood firm, convinced the last thing she wanted to be was a nun and, despite Father Powell's discouragement, began to look for a job in social service.

At this point, she recalled the offer of her fellow traveller Mrs Hardy of accommodation in Kansas and, with characteristic courage, set out alone on the arduous two-and-a-half-day journey west. On arrival, Grace soon discovered her new friend, who had never previously worked, was struggling to combine the demands of her job with the care of her two daughters, aged eight and two. At Mrs Hardy's suggestion, Grace applied to take over her post as Chief Travellers' Aid Assistant, allowing her to stay home with her daughters.* In order to do so, Grace had to face an interview panel which included the wife of the president of the railway company. She was successful at interview and later learnt the president had been anxious to employ an educated English woman whom he believed would be above bribery.

And so she began her new job looking out for unaccompanied women who, arriving in the third-largest railway station in the country, might find themselves bewildered by the vast space, which covered over 850,000 square feet. Her responsibility was to help them find loved ones, locate their onward destinations and advise them of safe lodgings within the city.[2]

The recently opened Union Station must have been an exhilarating place to work. Built in the Beaux-Arts style from limestone and granite, its two principal spaces were the Grand Hall, with a richly decorated and coloured coffered ceiling rising 95 feet above a polished marble

---

* The Travellers' Aid organization had been founded in 1907 with the aim of preventing single women being taken advantage of by unscrupulous predators when they travelled between American cities.

floor, and the North Waiting Hall, lit by vast segmental arched windows, which could accommodate 10,000 people.[3] Grace enjoyed working in this modern temple to travel, finding her new employment both interesting and exacting. One of her jobs was to make sure the grand public rooms were kept in good order, and she swiftly learnt the most effective way to deal with the hillbilly farmers who sat with their hobnailed boots on the seats. She recalled: "I began by being very English and very polite, saying 'Would you mind taking your feet off the seats'. They never took the slightest notice of me, and so then I got the lingo and said 'Hey brother! Get your feet off our three-hundred-dollar seats will you' and they would do it."

While there was much Grace enjoyed about her new life in America, her sense of social justice was outraged at the discrimination she found towards people of colour. She was ashamed when white people on the streetcars got up when a black person sat next to them and noted the black workers at the station, unlike their white colleagues, were let go without notice. When she was asked by the railway company president to collect back payments for laundry costs from the poorly paid black women employed as maids, she flatly refused, countering his angry reaction with the observation that one of the conditions of her employment was to inform him of anything she thought was not right at the station.

Her working day consisted of a double shift designed to coincide with the busiest times of travel—from 8 a.m. until 10 a.m. in the morning and 4 p.m. to 10 p.m. at night. As a consequence, she found it increasingly difficult to attend her Episcopalian church, which was situated some distance away. Seeking guidance from her parish priest, an elderly Virginian of Scottish extraction, he suggested to her surprise that she might attend the Roman Catholic church which was closer to the station: "If Almighty God can stay in a Roman Catholic Church for twenty-four hours a day, there ain't no reason why you shouldn't be there." Grace welcomed this pragmatic approach, and her early experience of ecumenism was to influence her stance on the issue throughout her life.

In the end, it was not her combative relationship with the president of the railway, the long hours or her unconventional church life that led her to leave Kansas, but rather the increasing awkwardness of her domestic situation. She began to feel trapped by Mrs Hardy's growing dependency, so in autumn 1915 made her escape.

She fled to the convent of the Community of St Mary, at Kenosha, Wisconsin, situated on the shores of Lake Michigan. Her choice of destination may have been facilitated by Lady Henry, who had spent time in the Midwest.[4] Grace made herself useful at St Mary's carrying out various domestic duties to support the work of the Sisters in the adjoining girls' school, Kemper Hall. Here, she noted wryly, many of the girls were from backgrounds of recently acquired wealth and may have been sent to the school not for the high standard of education, but to learn how to become ladies.

Life at St Mary's was a welcome break after the arduousness of her work in Kansas. Between her duties at the school, she took meals in silence with the Sisters in the dining room, the lack of conviviality more than compensated for by the magnificent views of the lake through the tall sash windows.[5] She welcomed the freedom of at least three free hours a day, which she spent at prayer in the chapel—reached by passing through a cloister, dimly lit by wall sconces and stained glass windows.[6] Originally built in the 1870s as a chapel for the school, the rather plain Gothic Revival structure had been enriched over the years through the generosity of former pupils. These improvements included a handsome hand-carved reredos and chancel screen from Germany and stained glass from London.[7]

Grace delighted in the magnificent surroundings of the school complex which, in addition to the convent and chapel, included an Italianate former mansion house, a four-storey gymnasium and an observatory with a striking metal domed roof, all set within 17½ acres of parkland on the lakeshore. St Mary's proved the perfect environment for her to live in community and develop her prayer life, without the commitment of being a fully-fledged Sister. However, despite all these positive features, her sense of restlessness returned. Reflecting later in life, she attributed these feelings to a change in attitude to the British after the outbreak of the First World War, with many Americans adopting a far from sympathetic stance. Consequently, after term ended in June 1916, she travelled east to Cape Cod, where she spent three months as a governess-companion to two young girls, before returning to England in the autumn.

In addition to her desire to return home, she began to experience an increasing sense of vocation. By this point, she had observed religious life in a variety of different forms: the missioning life of friar Father Andrew, the anchorites at Duxford, the small urban convent with its community service in Boston, and the teaching convent of St Mary's, Kenosha—none of whose practices she had felt drawn to join permanently. Consequently, almost by a process of elimination, she began to consider whether a more contemplative order might be what she was seeking and embarked on a correspondence with the Mother Superior of an enclosed community. Her mentor, Mother Ivy, who felt this type of community was entirely unsuited to Grace, vigorously discouraged this course of action. Her opinion was no doubt influenced by her experience of Grace's aptitude for social work. Her young protégé, however, in typical strong-willed fashion did not heed her concerns.

However, in the weeks before her departure for England she did begin to have misgivings—exacerbated by the unsatisfactory nature of the communications she was receiving from the Mother Superior. Her unease was compounded by an increasing preoccupation, which at that point she could only articulate as "a vague feeling after something I could not describe even to myself, which I had not seen any example of in any of the communities of which I had some experience".

The time came for her to leave, and on 9 September 1916 she set sail for England. Her passage in first class was paid for by the grateful parents of the girls from Cape Cod, who had been most impressed with her management of their headstrong girls. Despite the comfort of her berth, Grace would have been aware, two years into the First World War, of the dangers involved in the crossing—the SS *Arabic*, the ship on which she made her outward voyage, had been torpedoed the previous year with the loss of 44 lives.[8] However, despite several alarms during the voyage and an all-night delay on arrival, when the ship could not berth due to a mine alert, she arrived home safely.

Notes

1. Church of St John the Evangelist, "The Shrine on Bowdoin Street from 1883—1958", <https://floundah2013.wordpress.com/our-history/the-shrine-on-bowdoin-street-from-1883-1958-chapter-vii/>, accessed 18 May 2024.
2. E. Cimino, "The Travelers' Aid Society: Moral Reform and Social Work in New York City, 1907—1916", *New York History* (Summer/Winter 2016), <https://www.academia.edu/31095225/The_Travelers_Aid_Society_Moral_Reform_and_Social_Work_in_New_York_City_1907_1916>, accessed 19 May 2024, p. 35.
3. "Kansas City Union Station", Wikipedia (last modified 20 February 2024), <https://en.wikipedia.org/wiki/Kansas_City_Union_Station>, accessed 19 May 2024.
4. Black, *A Talent for Humanity*, p. 56.
5. "The Kemper Centre" [website] <https://kempercenter.com/history/ambrose-hall>, accessed 31 January 2021.
6. "The Kemper Centre" [website] <https://kempercenter.com/history/ambrose-hall>, accessed 31 January 2021.
7. "The Kemper Centre" [website] <https://kempercenter.com/history/ambrose-hall>, accessed 31 January 2021.
8. "SS *Arabic* (1902)", Wikipedia (last modified 30 April 2024), <https://en.wikipedia.org/wiki/SS_Arabic_(1902)>, accessed 19 May 2024.

CHAPTER 3

War and pacifism

On her arrival, Grace put all qualms about her choice of convent to one side, as she was confronted with the reality of a nation at war. Anxious to do something of use for her country, she faced a fresh dilemma. During her time in America, she had become convinced that she was a pacifist, and this conviction precluded her from enrolling in the Women's Auxiliary Army Corps or holding any position allied to the armed forces. Her eventual decision to join the recently formed Women's Police Service (WPS) she later described as "rather curious and somewhat (as I now think) inconsistent with my pacifist convictions".

Her decision may have been influenced by her recent experience as a Travellers' Aid assistant, as the work of the WPS included assisting women at railways stations.[1] Another factor may have been the continuing influence of Lady Henry, as the British Women's Temperance Association at that time was lobbying for women police "matrons" to ensure the protection of women when taken into custody.[2]

So Grace found herself close-cropping her hair, not to wear the cap and wimple of a religious novice, but as a requirement of the WPS, whose masculine uniform included a hard felt hat, dark blue belted jacket, ankle-length A line skirt and tall, black boots. She underwent training in first aid, self-defence, police-court procedure and signalling and was instructed to salute her superior female officers whilst addressing them as Sir.[3]

During the war, the Ministry of Munitions employed members of the WPS to police its factories, and in December 1916 Grace was sent to Gretna on the Scottish border, where women were employed at the vast national cordite factory built on 30 miles of moorland.[4] As part of her role, she was required to search women for metal items on their clothing such as hook-and-eye fastenings which could trigger an explosion, to supervise canteen and pay queues, search out malingerers and watch out for women who had collapsed from breathing in toxic substances.[5]

The task was daunting; she was just one of 37 policewomen attempting to bring order to the working lives of the 11,000 women workers. In the canteen, she witnessed women climbing over the counter to get to the food, and then starting food fights if it was something they did not like. She vividly recalled the experience:

> There were hundreds of girls, rough girls, Irish and Scots fishing lassies and other girls of that type ... not only were they wild and untrained, but cordite made them all in a constant state of over-excitement.

Paydays were similarly chaotic, taking hours longer than was necessary, as the women refused to form a queue. However, the atmosphere was more high-spirited than antagonistic, and within a month Grace and her fellow police officers had the girls forming orderly queues for their meals and pay, with anyone who argued sent to the back. She had a natural air of authority and was soon singled out along with a friend for additional duties patrolling the streets of Carlisle on Saturday nights. Here their task was to scoop off the street drunk male workers from the factory to prevent them from being robbed, before sending them back to the workers' hostel to sober up.

After four months, she was called to attend an inspection which took place in the first-class waiting room at Carlisle station. Grace noted disparagingly how one of the female officers insisted on being treated as if she were a man. Here she learnt that the chief police officer had a new post for her, and the next day she received a telegram with instructions to report to the chief constable of Oxford the following morning, 5 April 1917, at 10 a.m. Her new role was to help tackle the problem of prostitution in the city[6]—a growing issue recently identified by the moral welfare group the Oxford Watch Committee. Grace was chosen out of all the possible candidates as the committee's chairman, Sir Robert Buckle, had spent some time in Kansas City and was impressed by the reports of her work there. Consequently, she was given the pioneering post of Oxford's first woman constable.

She later recalled with wry amusement her first day at work when, on arrival at the police station, the elderly retired policeman on the front desk, who clearly had not been briefed on her appointment, "nearly fell off his perch" on learning who she was. Her new role presented many challenges: unlike her male colleagues, she had no powers of arrest and could only carry out her duties by trying to persuade offenders to go home, attempting a citizen's arrest or waiting for a male colleague.[7] Undaunted, she drew on her previous experiences in Kansas and Gretna. A contemporary photograph shows Grace on duty, striding down a busy shopping street with the purposeful and slightly self-conscious look of a newly appointed school prefect.

She soon realized that, as a woman, she was in a better position to carry out some of the duties her fellow male officers found challenging. These included the delicate matter of disputes over the Separation Allowance.[*] A number of soldiers had contacted the Soldiers' and Sailors' Families Association, who administered this allowance, requesting it should be terminated as their wives were pregnant and the child could not possibly be theirs. Through tactful negotiation and appeals for tolerance and forgiveness, Grace managed to get many of the allowances reinstated. Another area in which she made greater progress than her colleagues was in cases of child abuse. Here she was able to gain the confidence of young victims and piece together credible narratives that allowed cases to be brought to court.

Unfortunately, in addition to these aspects of her work, the discharging of which she found very rewarding, Grace was also required to enforce another duty that was anathema to her. This was the prosecution of the Defence of the Realm Act (DORA), which forbad women with venereal disease from having sexual intercourse with servicemen. She considered this legislation grossly unfair, as it criminalized the women only, and her stance led to a serious altercation with her chief inspector. She refused to arrest a prostitute under the Act and recalled the following scene, which

---

[*] The allowance was a percentage of a serviceman's pay, which was matched by the government and sent to his dependents.

took place in front of a number of other policemen: "Tindle [the chief inspector] then said to me 'You just mind your own business, we know what you think about this Act, the way I think, it's a very good Act' and I replied 'You would think so, damn fool that you are.'" Despite this act of gross insubordination, she kept her position and continued to police with her own methods: making friends with all the prostitutes and moving them on with firm but friendly insistence.

As an antidote to work, she began to retreat in her spare time into the fictional world of Joy Hooper—a regular contributor to *The Theosophical Review* who wrote under the pen name Michael Wood. Hooper wrote novels and short stories in the style of folklore, with the aim to express the mysticism of experience without religiosity. Meanwhile the pressures of policing DORA began to take their toll. Following an accident at work when she nearly drowned, Grace was shocked to find herself almost welcoming death and decided to resign her post after serving only 18 months.

Then followed a period of six months helping in a colony for women and girls who had been convicted of prostitution and theft. The women ranged from the mistresses of aristocrats to streetwalkers, and she vividly recalled the lively atmosphere of the place, which only on occasion descended into riot. As in Oxford, Grace treated the girls with friendliness and was known affectionately as Copette. She was not convinced that her work made much impact on the moral welfare of her charges but was satisfied that providing a safe environment and a sympathetic understanding of their situations was a useful service.

During this time, she began once more to be preoccupied by thoughts of a religious calling. Concluding the enclosed order she had previously considered was not the right place to test her vocation, she chose instead to return to Duxhurst, where Lady Henry had invited some of the nuns from the American Order of St Anne to live.[8] Here the Sisters led a life of religious devotion combined with a practical ministry assisting at the school for the children of the women inebriates.

She was received into the order on 25 August 1919 and took the religious name Teresa after St Teresa of Avila. Her decision to ally herself to the prominent sixteenth-century mystic was indicative of her continued interest in mysticism, which had by this point developed into a more conventional Christian form following her earlier interest in theosophy. Mysticism had been steadily growing in popularity amongst Christians in reaction at first to the fallout from Darwinism, and then to the horrors of the First World War. Many were drawn to its emphasis on direct personal experience, separate from the authority of the Church and the Bible, and books such as W. R. Inge's *Christian Mysticism* and Evelyn Underhill's *Mysticism* sold in high numbers.

Father Powell from Boston preached at her clothing ceremony and must have been delighted the young woman he had tried to encourage into the order in the States had finally found her religious home after four years of searching. He took as the text for his sermon the words spoken to Moses, "Speak to the Children of Israel that they go forward", using it to explore people's tendency to put caution in the way of adventure. His homily may or may not have been intended to pay tribute to the fearless nature of the new Sister Teresa. Whatever his intention, the words remained with her and over the years were to hold increasing significance.

There was much about her new life that appealed to the young novice: she got on well with the Sisters and was happy with the liturgical and devotional aspects of the life. In addition, the familiar rural surroundings, close proximity to her mentor, Mother Ivy, and the useful and rewarding work in the school, must all have been positive experiences. However, she was somewhat disquieted by the way the Mother Superior favoured her: the older woman was an artist and frequently asked Teresa to pose for her and allowed her to forgo some of the more arduous duties. In addition, she found the genteel approach of her fellow Sisters towards the unmarried mothers at the colony grating. When she spoke of her past experiences, which informed her more empathetic approach, she was told not to speak of such shameful matters in the house. After just one year, in the late summer of 1920, feeling increasingly like a misfit and troubled by the thought her vocation might lie elsewhere, she took the difficult decision to leave the order. Her superiors, who believed she had a genuine vocation, were dismayed by her decision, but she refused to be dissuaded.

Over the next two years, returning to secular life as Grace, she sought work in the familiar field of social work, where she found herself becoming part of the wider contemporary movement for social reform. Influenced by her experiences as a police officer and her time in the women's penal colony, she joined a campaign, which promoted a new approach to the rehabilitation of prisoners. Leading this movement was the Fellowship of Reconciliation (FoR), a non-denominational Christian group formed in the First World War to promote pacifism. Post-war, members of the organization had become involved in other causes, such as labour relations and the abolition of capital punishment,[9] and were planning a number of experimental projects designed to put their theories on the creation of social harmony into practice.[10]

One of these endeavours was a home for delinquent girls where the inmates could live rent-free while they learnt a trade, thus enabling them eventually to rejoin society. The scheme received the backing of the social campaigner and Labour MP, Dr Alfred Salter, who offered the use of his house Fairby Grange in Kent, which he had bought during the war as a convalescent home for conscientious objectors.[11] Other significant supporters of the Fairby Grange project included the judge Sir William Clarke Hall, who was magistrate of Old Street Juvenile Police Court, and Margery Fry and Cecil Leeson, honorary secretary and secretary respectively of the Howard League for Penal Reform.[12]

Grace heard about the project from her friends in the FoR and, following Home Office approval, was appointed warden.

Before Fairby Grange opened, she was asked to speak at a FoR conference to promote the new school. Here she met Father Bernard Walke, the charismatic Anglo-Catholic vicar of St Hilary in Cornwall. The two felt an immediate affinity, and she gladly accepted Walke's offer that he should become honorary chaplain to the school.

In addition to her connections in the FoR, Grace began to make her name within the Women's Freedom League (WFL)—an organization formed by those members of the suffragette movement who had taken a pacifist stance during the First World War. The organization held similar views to the FoR regarding penal reform—demanding progressive treatment rather than punitive punishment and opposing the death penalty.[13] Grace was invited to speak at meetings organized by the WFL and wrote for its newspaper *The Vote*.

In an article, "A New Experiment in Reformatory Work", published in *The Vote* in September 1921, she explained how the project at Fairby Grange would offer a new approach to dealing with young offenders. The article included a number of progressive ideas, including her theory that poor home environments led young people into crime, and the proposition that the harshness of the current system of reform had unintended negative consequences. She stated:

> I have known girls, who have made up their minds to steal no more because it doesn't pay, but who have left their reformatory with hardened hearts and bitter resentments against those who sent them to the school.

She advocated the provision of a happy home life for the girl offenders where they could be free to pursue their desires and longings, suggesting the thwarting of these feelings may have been the reason for their misdemeanours in the first place. She describes how the 20 girls accommodated at Fairby Grange would be encouraged to take a share in the management of school life, including the resolution of any conflicts which occurred.

Two months after the article was published, on 8 November 1921, the school opened, giving Grace the chance to put her theories into practice. Like the colony at Duxhurst, Fairby Grange housed its inmates in an idyllic setting—in this case an attractive seventeenth-century Kentish house complete with leaded casement windows and a mellow red peg-tiled roof studded with picturesque dormers. As at Duxhurst, the girls were offered training in horticulture, which was considered a good means of earning a living while increasing self-respect. At first, all went well and a notice from the inspecting education officer indicated the school was working satisfactorily.[14] True to his word, every couple of months Bernard Walke visited the school, making the long journey from the far west of Cornwall to Kent. Each time he visited, in addition to his duties as chaplain, he would stay a few nights, giving Grace the opportunity to share any concerns.

While she was at Fairby Grange she was asked by some of her fellow members of the FoR to join them in giving speeches at Hyde Park Corner.

Still outraged by the unfair attitude to women she had experienced due to the Defence of the Realm Act, she decided to speak on the moral responsibility of men regarding prostitution. Ironically, on her journey to Park Lane she was propositioned by a man on the bus, but this did not deter her from standing up in front of 200 men and stating baldly that any man using the service of a prostitute was every bit as deserving of judgement as the girls. At the end of her speech, there was silence before a spotty-faced man from the crowd piped up, "what would you say to a man whose doctor had told him that sexual indulgences were necessary for his health?" Quick as a flash she retorted that he should change his doctor, to roars of laughter from the crowd.

Meanwhile back in Kent, the shortcomings of the Fairby Grange experiment were beginning to become apparent. The premise of the enterprise—giving the girl offenders the advantages denied them by their deprived backgrounds and a degree of autonomy within a non-judgemental environment—was laudable. However, the FoR had woefully underestimated the disordered nature of some of the backgrounds of the inmates. There were no procedures for coping with misdemeanours, which inevitably led to an escalation of challenging behaviour that began with theft and absconding and culminated in a full-blown riot during which the telephone and electricity cables were cut. Grace felt she had no choice but to call the police, which resulted in the ringleader being taken into custody.

In despair, she wrote to Walke, explaining she did not feel able to continue at Fairby Grange, and he immediately responded, "Yes, well that's alright Grace, it's like a love affair, when it's over it's over, you can't do any more about it."

She consequently resigned from her post and not long afterwards, in July 1922, the school closed. The Home Office expressed regret at the closure, stating it believed the enterprise to be sound but acknowledging a lack of funds and a drop in inmate numbers (due to the increasing use of the probation system) meant closure was inevitable.[15]

The full implication of her decision to walk away from the project was not lost on Grace. She had spent two years planning and publicizing the work at Fairby Grange, during which she had made many influential contacts and earned a reputation as a significant voice in the world of social reform. She later recalled:

> This step was a costly and bewildering one, for I had no idea what to do next, I could only see that I had to relinquish active social work for God, and all that went with it, including a certain amount of public speaking which I had enjoyed and for which I had received praise and approbation.

In her confusion, she turned to Walke, who suggested she come to stay at St Hilary, where she could think over what her next move might be.

Notes

1. A. Woodeson, "The first women police: a force for equality or infringement?", *Women's History Review* 2:2 (1993), p. 226.
2. Woodeson, "The first women police", p. 218.
3. Clare Langley-Hawthorne, "The Women's Police Service During the First World War", <http://www.clarelangleyhawthorne.com/pdf/WPS_Background.pdf>, accessed 1 February 2021.
4. P. Clarke, *Hope and Glory Britain: 1900–2000* (London: Penguin, 2004), p. 94.
5. Woodeson, "The first women police", p. 227.
6. <https://www.thamesvalley.police.uk/police-forces/thames-valley-police/areas/au/about-us/who-we-are/thames-valley-police-museum/world-war-one-centenary/ww1---oxford-city-police/>, accessed 13 February 2021.
7. Woodeson, "The first women police", p. 224.
8. Black, *A Talent for Humanity*, p. 106.
9. G. G. J. den Boggende, "The Fellowship of Reconciliation 1914–1945" (PhD thesis, McMaster University, Hamilton, Ontario, 1986), p. 1.
10. den Boggende, "The Fellowship of Reconciliation", p. 332.
11. den Boggende, "The Fellowship of Reconciliation", p. 334.
12. den Boggende, "The Fellowship of Reconciliation", p. 334.

[13] C. L. Eustance, "'Daring to be Free': The Evolution of Women's Political Identities in the Women's Freedom League 1907–1930" (PhD thesis, University of York, York, 1993), p. 327.
[14] den Boggende, "The Fellowship of Reconciliation", p. 335.
[15] den Boggende, "The Fellowship of Reconciliation", p. 335.

CHAPTER 4

Four years at St Hilary

The far west of Cornwall has long been a place of retreat, its sense of otherness creating the perfect place to look back at the outside world and take stock. Grace arrived in springtime, when Cornwall is at its best, and as she travelled along the lane to the small churchtown of St Hilary, bordered with an avenue of trees planted by a former vicar, her spirits must have lifted. And equally uplifting would have been the prospect of spending time in the company of her dear friend Bernard Walke.

Walke was no ordinary country parson. A High Church Tractarian, he was initially viewed with great suspicion by some of his parishioners.[1] However, his sincerely held belief in social service, generosity of spirit and engaging demeanour soon endeared him to many. Those suspicious of the Catholic nature of his Holy Eucharist held in church were more than happy to join him at the open-air services on the downs to the south of the village on Sunday evenings. Dressed in a wide-brimmed hat and long black coat, he was an idiosyncratic sight travelling through the parish in a cart pulled by one of his beloved donkeys. Eschewed by the local gentry who were suspicious of his Christian Socialist sympathies and High Church practices,[2] Walke socialized instead with the nearby Newlyn School of artists, one of whom was his wife, Annie. Another, Laura Knight, affectionately described the Walkes:

> They were both long and thin, and Ber always wore dandy silk socks—he was not in the least like a parson to look at. A man with ideals that he lived up to—he was big-hearted enough to understand anyone and had it in him to enjoy vulgar fun as much as any. After we became intimate we often went to stay with the Walkes at St Hilary, as simple as any monastery in its furnishings.[3]

Walke's passionately held belief in pacifism, shared by Grace and many of his artist friends, drove him to work in areas where he felt peace and social harmony could be fostered. This led to him organizing aid for Russia (facing famine following the October Revolution), saying prayers for peace and reconciliation in Ireland[4] and attempting to reopen one of the many recently closed local mines through a mine workers' cooperative.[5] Consequently, when Grace arrived in the spring of 1922, she found at St Hilary a heady mix of Catholic ritual, artistic invention and socialist idealism.

Rather than sharing the monastic simplicity of the Walkes' vicarage, she chose to live in a cottage with two friends in the parish, spending much prayerful time in church, seeking guidance on the direction her life should now take. To begin with she felt she was being drawn towards a life not dissimilar to that of a friar—"a life of prayer, and a good deal of solitude, except for the summer and autumn months, when I would go off on an itinerating preaching tour, through villages in the west country. I thought I would speak on village green and in church halls and chapels if allowed to do so, and get my living by working for anyone who would give me food and a bed in return for help with the household chores." Her thoughts may have been influenced by an idea previously raised by Walke with the FoR in the immediate aftermath of the war. Influenced by J. M. Keynes' book *The Economic Consequences of the Peace*, he had proposed pairs of preaching friars should travel from community to community, living off the hospitality of others.[6]

Although Grace had already proved she had a gift for preaching during her time promoting Fairby Grange, she subsequently abandoned the idea, concluding she was not yet ready for such a form of life. Rather, she felt she would benefit from a period of obscurity and simple living in order to determine what her vocation should be. It is unclear whether she reached this decision through prayer or through guidance from Walke, who was now acting as her confessor.

However, her need for paid employment was pressing. After six weeks living in her friends' cottage, her money was running out, but she was desperate to stay in St Hilary, as she had grown to love the place. At this point, Walke offered a solution which would allow Grace to stay in the parish through utilizing a building to which he had been drawn ever since he arrived at St Hilary.[7] He suggested Grace take over the Jolly Tinners, a former inn close to the church, where she could look after children from the Fresh Air Fund. Walke and Annie were committed to helping youngsters, particularly those whose lives had been blighted by the war. Under a FoR scheme, they themselves had taken in two boys from Austria (a country on the brink of famine due to the continued Allied blockade).[8] Given Grace's former work as a governess and school warden, Walke would have assumed his young friend had the necessary skills for such an enterprise.

Grace, however, with characteristic determination and assurance, rather than follow Walke's suggestion, decided to pursue her own project for the Jolly Tinners. She enlisted the help of a friend, Miss Dickens, described by Walke as "Some lady unknown to me who had never been to St Hilary", to fund a children's home. Four suitable children were found by another of Grace's contacts, the London magistrate William Clarke Hall, with whom she had worked at Fairby Grange. Walke described the children two years later as "Clara, a beautiful wild creature, Billy a shy boy of twelve, Bill, the burglar, who was on two years' probation and Elizabeth a little girl of eight who had no parents or any other relatives we ever heard of".[9]

The Jolly Tinners provided a good base for the new enterprise with two sizeable reception rooms, one of which was the former bar, a kitchen to the rear with an old "Cornish slab" stove and four bedrooms upstairs which could be flexibly divided by sliding doors—this arrangement dated from the time the upper storey room was used as a club-room for the local miners.[10] In describing her first two years, Grace observed: "Things seemed to go smoothly, I looked after the children, trained the choir and did a number of church jobs. It was a fairly hard and exacting life, for the house was entirely un-modernized and I had only a little help. We were very poor and had to do without a good many things."

One of the "church jobs" referred to was supervising a prayer group for boys and girls known as The Children of Mary. Grace noted some of the children who attended this group were very able and suggested she might write a play for them to perform. Walke was delighted with the suggestion and offered to write the script for a nativity play. During the first rehearsals, Grace noted the children struggled with the formal language and suggested they be allowed to use their colloquial speech with which they were more comfortable. The suggestion was a great success: the play, which took place in atmospheric candlelight, was given an immediacy through the rich idiomatic language of the players as they moved through the church. In the audience for the second Christmas the play was performed were the theatre director Barry Jackson and the writer George Bernard Shaw. They were both greatly moved by the production and Jackson later approached Walke, who allowed the BBC to broadcast the production live on the radio on Christmas Eve 1927.

Working with Walke was undoubtedly inspiring and rewarding, but Grace found her day-to-day existence, running a house with only the most basic of conveniences and looking after four children from disadvantaged backgrounds, a significant challenge. At the end of two years, Miss Dickens informed her she could no longer fund the enterprise as she was going to get married and suggested the children should be dispersed to different institutions. Walke was scathing of the way this lady had tired of her experiment and was determined the home should continue.[11] He enlisted the help of his near neighbour Canon Rogers, the retired former rector of Penzance, and Mrs T. B. Bolitho, a local benefactor, who formed a committee to raise funds for the home. He was also eager for Grace to take in more children, which she reluctantly agreed to do in principle.

At the same time as her onerous domestic duties were increasing, Grace embarked on a period of deliberately sought asceticism: working without a salary and depending on the charity of others. She felt increasingly drawn to the life of St Francis of Assisi and was determined to carve out time each day, after the children had gone to bed, to pray in the church.

St Hilary is described by Pevsner as a "church of uncommon interest and arresting atmosphere".[12] The original thirteenth-century building had been almost completely destroyed by fire in the mid-nineteenth century, leaving only its tower and broach spire, visible from both north and south coasts, as a daymark for sailors. The main body of the church was rebuilt by William White, one of the leading architects of the Gothic Revival, to an unusual design incorporating shallow transepts whose junction with the nave forms a lantern lit by eight small windows giving a "low and mysterious light at the centre of the church".[13] What makes the church unique however is its sumptuous decoration carried out by friends of the Walkes from the Newlyn School, described by Pevsner as "a programme of enrichment that became and remains, the outstanding collection of early C20 religious art anywhere in Cornwall".[14]

The scheme began with painted wooden panels on the front of the choir stalls, the first of which was completed by Annie in 1917.[15] Walke described the work as "descriptive of the lives of Cornish saints, the collective work of Ernest Proctor, Dod Proctor, Annie Walke, Harold Harvey, Norman Garstin, Harold Knight, Alethea Garstin and Gladys Hynes".[16] These were some of the most noteworthy artists working in Britain during this period. By the time Grace was visiting the church for prayer, these extraordinary paintings were in situ. Each panel was in the style of the individual artist, the whole unified by their clarity and simplification[17] and a vibrant palette of crimson and cobalt blue, with further works of adornment in progress. Soon after its completion the historian Henderson described the reordering as transforming the "somewhat prim and Victorian interior with a vitality which is lacking in the more costly modern work of other churches".[18]

It was within this setting in the early spring of 1924 that Grace first experienced her calling to found a community. She had gone to the church one evening and found herself reflecting on her earlier idea of a life of preaching in poverty:

> As this thought came into my prayer it was made clear in the depth of my soul, as plainly as though the words had been spoken to me, that I must let the thought of living and praying solitarily go, that God wanted a group of people for this vocation, and a life in community.

Her initial reaction to this proposition was one of horror, as her previous experience of community life had left her with a strong desire never to see the inside of a convent again. However, as she continued in prayer, she experienced "a second soundless word to my soul. I was told that this group which was to be drawn round me, must live without fear, and without setting up the defence against other people with which religious communities safeguard the lives of their members."

Grace chose not to share this profound experience with Walke, despite the closeness of their relationship. This could be explained by his earlier refusal to take her commitment to a life of prayer seriously. When Grace had raised concerns that the increasing number of children at the Jolly Tinners would have a detrimental effect on her prayer life, his response was dismissive, observing he had never met anyone less suited than she to a life of prayer. They were also increasingly at odds over the running of the children's home, which Walke believed should be her priority. He himself was as committed as ever to the project of providing a stable home for the children sent by the London magistrates' court, describing movingly "little white faces searching the platform on their arrival at Penzance, grimy hands placed in mine as they arrive home".[19] Grace on the other hand was increasingly preoccupied by her experiences in the calm evening quiet of St Hilary Church, after the children had gone to bed.

Over the next few months, during her prayers, she saw a vision of a religious dress. She recalled: "The habit was brown, with some red on the front, and a white winged cap instead of the usual veil." Here her surroundings may possibly have provided a subliminal influence—the Cornish saints on the choir panels were mainly shown in religious dress with a white head covering, including a glamorous depiction of St Morwenna by Gladys Hynes. She continued to receive guidance in her prayers from spring through to early autumn, noting:

> Every time that some fresh direction was given me in prayer, the same thing happened, I was unable to reflect with my mind on what I had been told, I could only accept it and believe it had to happen when the time came.

Relations with Walke continued to deteriorate. He felt strongly that her decision not to accept a salary did not give her the right to act as she pleased. Furthermore, as her confessor, he sensed she was keeping something from him, but Grace was determined not to take him into her confidence:

> I could not at this point have said anything to him of what Our Lord has shown to me. I was sure he was not meant to have any part in the community when it began, and so could only say to him that I could not speak of what was in my heart.

So Grace kept her secret and it became a barrier between them, with both suffering physically and mentally as a consequence.

In mid-November, for the sake of Bernard's health, the Walkes went on vacation, leaving their maid Emma to help Grace at the Tinners during their absence. Emma took to joining Grace for evening prayer in the church after the children were asleep. On the night of 21 November 1924 (the Feast of the Presentation of Our Lady), the two women were preparing to make the short walk to church when Grace noticed a glowing light through the tall landing window of the Tinners illuminating the surrounding fields. Suspecting a fire, she called Emma. The women hurried into the lane to locate the source of the blaze and encountered a tall pillar of light immediately adjacent to the house. Grace later described the incident in detail:

> At the side of the house there was a gigantic figure, veiled and crowned in a dazzling, perfectly still light. The figure seemed to reach from the sky to the ground. It was the figure of a woman but we saw no features, the face, as well as the rest of the figure, was veiled in the pure light. We could see each other's faces and the hedges in the lane, and the fields beyond the lane, quite clearly in this light. The figure did not move at all, though we stood silently watching it for nearly ten minutes. It was still there when we left and walked up to the church, but there was no sign of it when we returned in about three-quarters of an hour.

Strangely, neither woman spoke to the other of the event for a long time afterwards, but Grace became convinced what they had witnessed was a vision of "Our Lady of the Light", which she interpreted as an affirmation of her calling to found a community.

Any thoughts about her future, however, were on hold as, following the incident, her health broke down again and further surgery was required.

She travelled to the Royal Free Hospital in London to be examined by a woman surgeon who was later to become a friend. Although she was clearly unwell, Walke insensitively suggested Grace could, while she was in London, collect four children to add to the number at the Jolly Tinners. Grace had reservations about taking on the two boys and two girls who were from a very bad home and felt they ought to be separated. Walke thought otherwise, so Grace and all the children returned to St Hilary. This made the six weeks before her operation extremely difficult, as she tried, not entirely successfully, to settle them in.

In addition to her concerns about the new children, Grace had another pressing problem—given she was no longer drawing a salary, how was she going to pay for her surgery? Approaching Walke was not an option, as, although she knew him to be most generous, the tensions between them made such a request impossible. Fortunately, a cheque for £25 sent by a friend enabled her to set off on 17 March for her operation and subsequent three-week stay in hospital. By the time she left, things had become so bad at home that she found her post-operative weeks "a time of great grace and inner peace, which no pain or discomfort could really touch".

On leaving hospital, she went to Sussex to stay with the same friend who had paid for her surgery. While she was convalescing, her friend told Grace about the apparition of Our Lady at Llanthony Abbey in Wales—a monastery created in 1869 by the eccentric Father Ignatius. The sighting described by her friend was experienced by a group of young boys in the summer of 1880 in a meadow adjoining the monastery and was reported to the *Hereford Times* by Father Ignatius as follows:

> The figure was dressed in a white alb, only the sleeves were wider than alb sleeves. The hands were both raised, and from head to feet, a dazzling white light, oval shape was shining round the body.[20]

Grace was immediately struck by the similarities with her own vision and by the connection with Father Ignatius. She had met this clergyman once when he preached at her local church in Hastings, and the encounter had left a lasting impression on her as she felt he had seen into the state of her soul and had prayed for her.

Encouraged by these connections, Grace shared with her friend her own experience of the Lady of Light, and the instructions she had been receiving regarding the founding of a community. The friend suggested she talk over her experiences with her spiritual director, Father Lucius Cary. He, like Father Powell in Boston, was a member of the Society of St John the Evangelist and had himself been involved in the development of a new community. Father Cary's community, the contemplative order of The Sisters of the Love of God, had been founded in 1907. He was appointed their Chaplain General in 1914 and charged with helping the Sisters write a Rule of Life and form a Constitution, making him well-placed to offer Grace advice.[21]

Grace was initially reluctant to share her plans, perhaps worried about a sceptical reaction, perhaps trepidatious of the inevitable momentum such a revelation would generate. On the first count, her fears proved unfounded:

> He listened very kindly and attentively as I outlined what I believed God had shown me, including the village missioning and open-air meetings, as part of the vocation of the community to come. When I finished speaking, there was a grave silence, which I broke by saying rather nervously 'Do you think all this sounds impossible, Father'. To which he replied 'Not impossible, my daughter, only very difficult'.

An awkward situation then developed as Father Cary went on to discourage Grace's friend from joining her in her endeavours. This resulted in the friend becoming less encouraging, suggesting Grace could not expect anyone to believe she had received a revelation from God. By this point, however, Grace refused to be deterred, maintaining God *did* speak to ordinary people like herself. Seeking further validation she turned to her old mentor Mother Ivy, who confirmed that what she had witnessed was indeed a vision of Our Lady of Light.[22]

On returning to Cornwall, Grace's plans had to be put on hold as more pressing matters required her attention. She was staying at the home of Mrs Bolitho, one of the members of the Jolly Tinners committee, to continue her convalescence and was informed all had not been well with the children during her absence. When she eventually returned to the house in mid-June, she found filthy conditions with the children clearly upset.

Recovering from her operation and facing the added challenge of new charges who had clearly not integrated well, Grace decided to act on a suggestion made to her by Mother Ivy. She had been told by a priest in Scotland about a young woman, Jean Barbour, who wished to live a life of poverty, prayer and labour. Mother Ivy suggested Jean could be a like-minded and helpful contact. Grace was keen to act on this suggestion as, in the short term, an extra pair of hands at the Jolly Tinners was desperately needed and, in the long term, such a young woman might be interested in her idea of forming a community. Walke, however, immediately perceived the potential for the latter and refused to allow Jean to join her. His fears were well founded as Grace had already begun to attract a growing circle of young girls in the parish, who attended meetings with her to discuss living a life of prayer.

However, by September, possibly in recognition of the challenges she faced with her charges, Walke capitulated and Jean came to stay. Any thoughts Grace might have had of Jean improving life at the Jolly Tinners were short-lived. She describes the winter of 1925 as the hardest they had experienced. Jean, from a wealthy family and unused to domestic work, proved to be little practical help and, more worryingly, began to show signs of an erratic temperament. Grace herself was not in good health and her relationship with Walke further deteriorated. Undeterred, she continued to lay the foundations for forming a community; in addition to the meetings at the Tinners, some of the local girls now joined her for her evening prayer in the church, and she discussed with Jean the possibility of acquiring a cottage which could potentially provide a base for the new community. It was important to her they remained in St Hilary—the place where she had received her calling and experienced her vision.

There was, however, a major obstacle to this plan in the form of Walke. He had already made his feelings plain regarding Grace's unsuitability for the life of a religious and was passionately committed to the cause of the children's home. To add to his frustrations, one of the young women Grace had attracted was his own maid Emma Curnow, whom he mentions several times in his book *Twenty Years at St Hilary*. Emma was close to the Walkes and in some respects was more like a member of the family than a servant. When they arranged a fancy dress party one Christmas Eve, which included some of the famous artists from the Newlyn School, Emma was invited to attend along with a number of her own friends.[23] The thought of losing his matron and maid, and having their new enterprise on his doorstep, was too much for Walke to countenance and an extreme enmity soured the relationship of the two former friends.

In addition to the undoubted strength of her religious vocation, one cannot help but suspect a further factor in the situation was Grace's lack of vocation for the care of young children. It is through *Walke* that we learn the names of her charges and their backgrounds. In her own account of the St Hilary years, the children are referred to only in terms of their needs and the problems arising from their background. Compare this with Walke's observations of life at the children's home made ten years later:

> There is protection and security, a place where dinner is always ready when they return from school and where there is some one who has time to stop and listen to their tales of what they have been doing. Add to this the long summer days spent on the beach at Perran, and winter evenings round the slab in the kitchen, and you will have some kind of picture of the life that goes on at the Jolly Tinners.[24]

By Lent 1926, Grace had decided, in order to avoid an irretrievable breakdown in their relationship, she would have to give up the struggle of trying to make a success of the children's home. Walke, equally determined Grace should not trial her new community in his parish, suggested that she try Blisland, a small village on Bodmin Moor with an Anglo-Catholic priest and a church he knew would appeal to her. And so it was that on 13 May, Jean and Emma set off for their new life, with Grace noting ruefully that everyone was heartily glad to see her go and even the children seemed entirely indifferent to her leaving.

She later recalled what a dreadful wrench it was to walk away: "for I loved the church and everything at St Hilary more I think, than I have ever, or shall love any place, and I loved Bernard deeply, and I knew that, underneath all his unkindness and determination to oppose me, he loved me too, there was an affinity between our souls which was never really broken."

Notes

1. D. Allchin, *Bernard Walke: A Good Man Who Could Never be Dull* (Abergavenny: Three Peaks Press, 2000), p. 10.
2. H. Miles Brown, *The Church in Cornwall* (Truro: Oscar Blackford Ltd, 1964), p. 110.
3. The Cornwall Artists Index, "Annie Walke", <https://cornwallartists.org/cornwall-artists/annie-walke>, accessed 3 April 2021.
4. Allchin, *Bernard Walke*, p. 14.
5. Allchin, *Bernard Walke*, p. 17.
6. den Boggende, "The Fellowship of Reconciliation", p. 337.
7. B. Walke, *Twenty Years at St Hilary* (Truro: Truran, 2002), p. 190.
8. den Boggende, "The Fellowship of Reconciliation", p. 312.
9. Walke, *Twenty Years at St Hilary*, p. 191.
10. Walke, *Twenty Years at St Hilary*, p. 190.
11. Walke, *Twenty Years at St Hilary*, p. 191.
12. P. Beacham and N. Pevsner, *The Buildings of England, Cornwall* (New Haven and London: Yale University Press, 2014), p. 550.
13. Beacham, *Cornwall*, p. 550.
14. Beacham, *Cornwall*, p. 550.
15. J. Rendell, *Cornish Churches* (St Teath: Bossiney Books, 1982), p. 41.
16. Walke, *Twenty Years at St Hilary*, p. 106.
17. C. Fox, *Painting in Newlyn 1900–1930* (Penzance: Newlyn Orion, 1985), p. 79.
18. C. Henderson, *The Cornish Church Guide and Parochial History of Cornwall* (Truro: D Bradford Barton Ltd, 1925), p. 83.
19. Walke, *Twenty Years at St Hilary*, p. 195.

[20] H. Allen, *New Llanthony Abbey: Father Ignatius's Monastery at Capel-y-ffin* (Shrewsbury: YouCaxton, 2016), pp. 255–6.
[21] E. Pendleton, "To God and God Alone: The Contemplative Communities Celebrate Centenaries", *Cowley Magazine* (Autumn 2006), <https://issuu.com/ssje/docs/cowley_autumn_06/11>, accessed 19 April 2021.
[22] Correspondence with Mother Mary Agnes of SOLI.
[23] Walke, *Twenty Years at St Hilary*, p. 140.
[24] Walke, *Twenty Years at St Hilary*, p. 197.

CHAPTER 5

Blisland—"This holy and peaceful place"[1]

Whatever Walke's motivations in dissuading Grace, Emma and Jean from forming their nascent community within his own parish, he undoubtedly had their best interests at heart when he encouraged them to go to Blisland. The rector, Father Ernest Clarabut, had trained him as a young curate in Walthamstow,[2] and Walke knew his High Churchmanship would appeal to Grace. Similarly, Father Clarabut would not view her desire to form a new religious community with suspicion. Walke would also have known she would respond well to the natural and architectural delights of the village. A village on Bodmin Moor conjures up a visual picture of blasted heath, wind-twisted trees, cowering cottages and a draughty, unloved church. Indeed, Blisland is only five miles away from Bolventor, the setting for Daphne du Maurier's Gothic *Jamaica Inn*. However, its secluded setting on the north side of a river valley, at a relatively low height compared to many of the surrounding moorland settlements,[3] gives Blisland a gentle picturesque character noted by Pevsner: "The churchtown is grouped prettily around a treed green."[4] The large green space at the heart of the village, typical of many Saxon settlements but rare in Cornwall, is surrounded by low granite cottages and notable seventeenth-century houses whose charms were favourably described by A. L. Rowse: "a grey granite village around a green" with "not one ugly building in it".[5]

If the picturesque nature of the village helped to console Grace for the loss of her beloved St Hilary, the village church must have provided an even greater source of solace. Betjeman enthused: "Of all the country churches of the West I have seen I think the church of St Protus and St Hyacinth, Blisland, in Cornwall, is the most beautiful."[6] The original Norman church had been extended in the fifteenth century to include transepts, south aisle and a tower unusually positioned adjoining the north transept. The medieval wagon roof with its carved ribs and bosses is magnificently complemented by an inspired programme of restoration by the architect F. C. Eden at the end of the nineteenth century. Betjeman praised his "amazingly rich screen and loft which extends the whole width of the church, a blaze of red and gold and green and white, with a rood over its centre", which he described as giving "an unforgettable sense of joy and mystery".[7] Beyond the screen, the high altar is described by Pevsner as "in the Italian Renaissance style, oddly incongruous yet wholly successful in its glinting gold presence" and the "resultant effect of the whole interior being one of numinous luminosity... captivating in its recreation of the character and atmosphere of the medieval church".[8]

By the time the three companions arrived in Blisland, the village had already developed from an isolated rural settlement into a holiday destination. In addition to the cottages accommodating rural workers and quarrymen from the nearby De Lank Quarry and the usual assortment of services in the form of a grocer, post office, blacksmith and carpenter, the picturesque setting and proximity to the railway station at Bodmin Road meant that by 1910 the local pub, Ye Royal Oak Inn, was described in Kelly's Directory as "good accommodation for cyclists and anglers". We do not know which of the small cottages the women chose for their home, but we do know how they paid for it: Grace recalled Jean was the only one with money, enjoying an income of £140 a year from her family.*

Inside they furnished the cottage with a few cheap pieces and set up an oratory in the sitting room. Most of their religious observances, however, took place in the beautiful surroundings of the church, where Father Clarabut was happy for them to say the Day Hours and where they accompanied him at Mass. In addition, they had a strict rule of silence, said the whole of the rosary daily and spent two hours a day in individual prayer. Grace decided to return to her religious name of Teresa and finally felt able to devote herself to the spiritual life previously denied her through the necessity of daily work.

All, however, was not entirely well and very quickly the three women began to experience some of the disadvantages of living a communal life.

---

* The equivalent of nearly £10,000 today.

At the heart of the difficulties lay the balance of power: Teresa had the vision, experience and probably the superior intelligence of the three; Emma, a simple country girl, was a natural acolyte; Jean had the financial clout and the assumption of authority this can bring. To Teresa's dismay it soon became apparent that Jean felt she should be in charge, recruiting Emma's support and insisting decisions regarding the community should be made by the assent of the majority. Although this was a source of concern to Teresa, who had recognized Jean's mental instability at St Hilary and feared some of the idiosyncratic practices she proposed were more suited to a cult than a religious order, her initial reaction was one of patience and hope that the two would begin to see reason.

Jean and Emma ignored Teresa's suggestions for a fair division of labour and used their majority position to allocate the household tasks in their favour. Things began to descend into farce when Jean proposed everything within the community should be shared, including their clothes. This idea was ignored by Teresa but adopted with enthusiasm by Emma. The former maid, who had never previously had anything of quality to wear, could not resist the beautiful designs and rich fabrics of Jean's clothes. This culminated in Jean discovering all her silk slips and most of her dresses had been purloined, and the resulting heated argument ended the clothes sharing experiment.

As the summer wore on, Teresa became increasingly concerned they would struggle to function effectively as a group—even for the initial year they had originally agreed upon. Despite not having much else to do, both Jean and Emma began to baulk at the requirements of the rule of prayer and office, saying it was too much for them. Feeling unwell, Jean decided to return to Scotland for a few weeks to recuperate and to meet with her confessor, Father Robert Andrews, the priest who had suggested she should join Teresa at St Hilary. Emma and Teresa duly travelled to the station in Truro to see Jean off. Just as the train was leaving the station she leant out of the window to ask if Teresa would be willing to move to Scotland if Father Robert agreed to them living in his parish. Seeing this as a potential way out of what had become an impossible situation, Teresa instinctively agreed. Later, examining her reaction, she decided some priestly authority might be just what was needed to curb Jean's more outré ideas and impart some discipline into Emma.

Meanwhile, Teresa learnt from Mother Ivy that Father Robert was about to take up the post of vicar of Holy Trinity, Paisley. Furthermore, he was to be joined in his parish by a young woman, Margaret Pearce, who had a similar interest to Teresa's in pursuing a form of religious life without joining an existing community. Margaret had been a concert pianist who had married a fellow pianist of some repute. After the death of the man she not only loved but greatly admired, she decided to walk away from the artistic life they had shared to devote herself to the service of God.[9]

Father Robert, on hearing from Jean about her communal life at Blisland, proposed she and her companions might consider joining Margaret in Paisley. He suggested he and Margaret should travel to Blisland to meet Teresa and Emma in order to determine whether they might be compatible, and in the meantime Jean remained in Scotland visiting relatives.

Father Robert and Margaret arrived on 20 August 1926, in torrential rain, which did not let up for the entire 24 hours of their stay in Blisland. As soon as Teresa and Margaret met, each knew they had found a soul mate. Teresa described the encounter:

> She came down with Father Robert and spent the night with us and this is one reason why I always loved her so much; she had never seen me before, but by the morning she was just absolutely prepared to put herself and her whole life into whatever it was I was going to do, even if she knew nothing about it.

Alongside this heady encounter was the bathetic figure of Emma, whose latest whimsical fancy had led her to cut her own hair with such disastrous results she wore a handkerchief wrapped around her head for the duration of Margaret's visit.

Teresa was most impressed that, while Father Robert stayed in the spacious nineteenth-century rectory, Margaret opted to join her and Emma in their cottage undismayed by the austerity of their surroundings. Furthermore, her enthusiasm to join them in church at 6.30 a.m. to recite Lauds, Prime and part of the rosary was a welcome contrast to the increasing reluctance shown by Emma and Jean to carry out these devotions. The previous night they had stayed up late, with Margaret describing the tiny flat she had taken in a Paisley tenement and Teresa outlining the type of community she believed God had called her to form. When Father Robert joined the women at the cottage the following morning, they continued their discussion on the feasibility of Teresa, Jean and Emma joining Margaret to live and work together under Father Robert's direction. Teresa voiced her concern that Margaret would be sharing the accommodation she had chosen for herself with three other women, to which Father Robert replied: "She'll not like it, but if she thinks it is the Will of God she will do it." And so it was decided. Margaret would move into the flat on 8 September with the others joining her ten days later.

Teresa and Emma stayed on in the cottage at Blisland until the end of August, using their time productively making jam and jelly from the rectory garden fruit. Emma then went to St Hilary for a fortnight to see her family and Teresa left to join Jean at one of her beautiful family homes in Perthshire.

Teresa had hoped the time at Blisland would be an interlude during which, through prayer and meditation, they would discover what their next move should be. In this respect the project had been a success, but it had also raised some concerns in her mind about the suitability of Jean and Emma for the religious life. However, buoyed up by her meeting with Margaret and the involvement of Father Robert, who would bring an authority and legitimacy that could underpin their endeavours, she left Cornwall confident the formation of a new type of religious community could be achieved.

Notes

[1] John Betjeman, *Collins Guide to English Parish Churches* (London: Collins, 1958), p. 119.
[2] H. Keast, *The Catholic Revival in Cornwall* (Helston: CAC, 1983), p. 17.
[3] Bridget Gillard, *Blisland Conservation Area Appraisal* (NCDC, 2007), p. 3.
[4] Peter Beacham and Niklaus Pevsner, *The Buildings of England, Cornwall* (New Haven and London: Yale University Press, 2014), p. 102.

5   Gillard, *Blisland*, p. 13.
6   John Betjeman, *Cornwall* (London: John Murray, 1988), p. 59.
7   Betjeman, *Collins Guide*, p. 119.
8   Beacham and Pevsner, *Cornwall*, p. 101.
9   Information from correspondence with Mother Mary Agnes.

CHAPTER 6

A pattern of living in Paisley

The new start in Scotland began with melodrama. On 18 September 1926, Teresa and Jean set out on the 100-mile journey from Jean's family holiday home in Inverness-shire to Paisley; Jean was in floods of tears behind the wheel because she did not think that the life they were about to embark on would be hard enough. Depression followed melodrama as they eventually turned into the noisy urban street of tall sandstone shops and houses where they were to live. A greater contrast with the peaceful, rural idylls of St Hilary and Blisland could not be found.

Their new home at 15 Well Meadow was reached by climbing three flights of a circular stone staircase. Teresa mounted with increasing despair, her mood only somewhat lifted at the top by the sight of the distant Gleniffer Braes parkland and Margaret, who had prepared tea. The warm welcome and the rural view could not, however, detract from the limitations of their accommodation. The "room and kitchen", as it was known, consisted of a bedroom, quickly christened "the ice-box", a tiny boxroom and a small kitchen, which accommodated a "bed in the wall", a sink and the coalbunker. There was no hot water or bath, and they had to share a lavatory with the people in the flat opposite. Teresa and Jean shared the bedroom, Emma was to sleep in the kitchen and Margaret on a mattress on the floor of the boxroom. During the day, the mattress was lifted and the tiny room became an oratory. Any concerns they may have been feeling about the lack of space cannot have been helped by the arrival of Father Robert on their first evening. He came with news that Mother Ivy had written to him observing their enterprise would be "fatal" if they did not have separate bedrooms.

The following day Emma arrived from Cornwall and the four women immediately began their ordered life of prayer. This involved reciting all

47

the Day Hours, some of which were said in the parish church of Holy Trinity which was ten minutes' walk away. Built in 1833, Holy Trinity was one of the first Episcopalian churches built in Scotland, and its plain largely unadorned interior would have presented a stark contrast to the decorative splendours of Blisland and St Hilary were it not for its elaborately decorated chancel with marble and alabaster reredos inserted in 1884 by the Earl and Countess of Glasgow.[1]

Each morning at 6.30 a.m., the women set out to recite Lauds and Prime at the church, followed by Mass at 7.30 a.m. and then Terce, after which they would walk home for breakfast. The office of Sext was said wherever they were at that time of the day, and then they would return to church after lunch to say None. In the early days, they went to church again later in the afternoon to say Vespers, before finally ending the day back at church for Compline. As time went by, they decided Vespers could be said at home, but still spent an hour a day walking back and forth, whatever the weather.

Paisley in the 1920s, thanks to the wealth generated by the thriving textile industry and the consequent philanthropy of the industry's magnates, had developed into a prosperous and thriving town with a phalanx of handsome civic and cultural buildings in an attractive mix of Gothic Revival, Classical, Art Nouveau, Neo-Renaissance and Art Deco styles. From its lively skyline of gables, spires and turrets to its wide streets lined with blonde and red sandstone tenements, embellished with cast and wrought ironwork, the town centre presented a confident and thriving aspect.

In contrast, the poorer districts, which included Well Meadow, were very run-down and deprived. Most of the families, some with large numbers of children, lived in two rooms with no lavatory. Teresa later recalled: "The majority of the families who sent their children to our Sunday school lived in over-crowded homes and real poverty."

Dressed in a sober uniform of navy-blue dresses and raincoats, plain black hats and black stockings, the four women became a familiar sight moving about the parish undertaking the tasks assigned to them by Father Robert. In addition to the Sunday school, they ran a junior Bible class, for which Teresa was deputed to teach the children with the greatest learning difficulties, and a teacher training class. They visited regularly throughout the parish, getting to know most of the church congregation, and held meetings for local women, encouraging those in better circumstances to help out their less fortunate sisters. They took it in turns to carry out their own domestic work, with one pair having a fortnight of housework, cooking and washing while the other pair focused on parish duties. The housework was hard and time-consuming, especially the laundry which took place in a communal facility that was part of the tenement. Thursday was their allotted laundry day, and a Roman Catholic woman in the building, who was sympathetic to their devotional needs, kept the copper fire alight while they attended Mass in the morning and fetched in their washing if it began to rain, as was quite frequently the case.

Teresa deliberately chose Emma as her partner in the domestic work, as she felt she could best control the young woman if she began to play up. Things went smoothly for the first two weeks. Emma, as a former maid, was in familiar territory, and Teresa was used to such work. The next fortnight, however, was less of a success. Both Jean and Margaret had grown up with maids, and while Margaret was more than happy to learn what was required, Jean was determined to do things her own way, dissolving into tears if challenged.

In addition to their parish duties and regular prayer commitments, the women's lives were organized to reflect that of a religious community, with the final decision on how they could behave resting with Father Robert. They required his permission to have visitors, to visit anyone who was not a parishioner, and to fast. Father Robert would have been aware the original impetus to set up an order had come from Teresa, but he was keen for the women to operate as equals. Furthermore, he was unwilling to accept Teresa as an authority figure. While having absolute confidence in the vocation of Margaret and a wary admiration for the fervid expressions of faith from Jean, there was something about Teresa which provoked in him a reaction similar to that of Bernard Walke. He too doubted whether Teresa had a vocation to a life of prayer.

The austerity of their domestic lives and the arduous nature of the parish work soon began to tell on Jean's fragile mental health. This took the form of an increasing obsession with living a life of exaggerated holy poverty. She adopted irrational stances such as a passionate opposition to the purchase of a much-needed clothes wringer and a bitter objection to hot lemon drinks being provided when one of the women had a cold. She argued incessantly with Teresa, even on the rare Saturday afternoons when they took time off to drive into the countryside. At the wheel of her old Ford, Jean would spend the time weeping and upbraiding Teresa as the car skidded between the banks of the country roads and clipped the curbs of pavements.

In early 1927, after several months of increasing tension, Margaret went to Father Robert and asked for Teresa to be given authority over the others with the hope this might subdue some of Jean's antagonism. Father Robert agreed Teresa could have authority regarding the material side of their lives, but not in spiritual matters. Unfortunately, the new hierarchy, if anything, exacerbated the situation. Jean tried to undermine Teresa's confidence by relating to her unfounded criticisms she alleged had come from Margaret. More damagingly, she began to spread untruths about Teresa to Father Robert, further undermining their relationship. When, in exasperation, Teresa expressed her concern to him that Jean was clearly unwell, he responded fiercely that Jean would be worth ten of her if she could only get her prayer life right.

Tensions between Teresa and Jean continued to build, resulting at the end of April in a shocking incident. Both women had gone to their shared room at 9.30 p.m. having returned from church after the last office of the day. As Teresa closed the door, Jean pushed her against it, gripped her wrists and proceeded to harangue her for several hours. Teresa recalled that she "dared not struggle with her, she was a tall and strongly made person—and I knew that if I moved she would be violent". Eventually Jean calmed down and went to bed, but the following morning at Mass, still in shock, Teresa broke down in tears. Father Robert, finally realizing something was very wrong, agreed Jean should go back to her family in Edinburgh. Teresa later learned Jean's family had already raised concerns over her wellbeing and were anxious for her to return.

Father Robert put the blame for Jean's poor mental state and the need for her to leave Paisley firmly at Teresa's door and insisted she should do penance. She agreed to fast for two days, having only tea and a slice of bread in the morning and the same again in the evening. On the second day of her fast, Teresa and Margaret were required to go into Glasgow for some shopping. During the tram journey into the city, Teresa began to feel faint and was only prevented from collapsing by Margaret. She led her friend to the nearest department store tearoom and, to the strains of a live band, they had a substantial afternoon tea. The incident is illustrative both of the growing friendship and solidarity between the two women but also Teresa's increasing trust in her own judgement. Not only was she prepared to defy the strictures of Father Robert, but she would have fun in so doing.

The requirements of parish and domestic work increased after the departure of Jean, and Emma became increasingly despondent. Her attitude to the whole enterprise had been one of experiment and adventure, but the rather grim realities of life in Paisley began to take their toll. Things came to a head when Teresa and Margaret took on the end-of-life care of a local cobbler's wife who was dying of Bright's disease. The women were out all night and Emma had been deputed to provide tea when they returned exhausted at 6 a.m. Each morning she overslept and failed to fulfil her task. Eventually the three women sat down together and came to the mutual conclusion that Emma was not suited to the venture. She headed back to her more congenial life in Cornwall but continued to maintain a friendship and correspondence with both Teresa and Margaret.

Following Emma's departure, the two remaining women moved closer to the church to lessen the time spent walking back and forth, but increasingly felt over-burdened by their parish commitments. In September 1927, they made a promise of obedience to Father Robert, which Teresa later regretted, noting: "The promise should have been to obey our Rule, not to obey a person." Just as with Walke in Cornwall, Teresa began to find herself increasingly in conflict with her parish priest. Father Robert's interest in the women was their parish work, while Teresa remained preoccupied with the idea of forming a religious community and the necessity of prioritizing their prayer life. Furthermore, Father Robert was devoted to Margaret, but suspicious of Teresa—partly as a result of Jean's accusations but also due to criticisms he had heard about her from another person in the parish with whom he was close.

It is interesting to speculate just what it was about Teresa that made first Walke and then Father Robert so sure she was not the right person to pursue a life of prayer, much less to head a religious order. There was no doubting the strength of her convictions, but it was perhaps this quality of strength which they reacted against. In the late 1920s, obedience in women would still have been considered a virtue by most men, and an important tenet of the religious life. Moreover, among the churchgoing population, the clergyman was a figure of authority whose opinions would rarely be questioned. Teresa, in contrast, would query and even disobey the orders of her parish priest if she did not think they accorded with what God had called her to do.

There was also the question of class. Margaret and Jean were from upper middle-class backgrounds and, although Jean could display erratic behaviour, they both had the manners and speech of ladies. Emma, with her West Country burr and practical ability, was clearly working class. Teresa on the other hand was an anomaly. Despite her illegitimate past, she had reinvented herself through travel, work, study and some very advantageous connections into a redoubtable individual. If even Walke, with his wide circle of artistic and literary connections, found her difficult to handle, it is unsurprising that Father Robert also struggled. Looking back on their relationship, Teresa pondered whether their lack of empathy was due to her Englishness: "He found me very difficult to understand and that isn't surprising, for at that time he knew very few English people, and I think didn't like them as a race." More probable was her other conclusion: "He realized that something in me, my vocation in fact, was in silent opposition to him all the time, and he was not used to being opposed in that particular way."

Despite the domestic challenges and uneasy relations with their priest, Teresa and Margaret managed to carry out some significant acts of service within the community, including supporting the destitute and sick. There were moments of joy too, especially some "lovely outings" with the children, including springtime visits to a local bluebell wood. Both women, however, were aware Father Robert continued to be suspicious of Teresa and her ambitions. This antipathy, in addition to the stress of the hard work and poverty of their day-to-day living conditions, began to tell on Teresa's health. She recalled: "I began to be quite frequently exhausted and early in 1928, was in bed for ten days and was ordered away for a rest by the doctor, who said I was suffering from brain fog and complete over tiredness." She returned home after three weeks, but it was clear she was not yet ready to return to her parish duties. Respite came from an unusual quarter. Jean had returned from a year in Canada in much better shape both mentally and physically and invited Teresa to join her and her family for a holiday at their second home in Inverness-shire.

Being away from Paisley gave Teresa the space and perspective to reflect on her situation, but this only left her with an increasing feeling of confusion. On the one hand she greatly admired Father Robert, later acknowledging "the light and grace he had been instrumental in bringing to my soul", and also describing him as a "spiritual genius". However, she could not ignore the fact that the vocation she fervently believed God had called her to during those long nights of prayer at St Hilary ran in opposition to Father Robert's wishes. Mindful of the force and charisma of his personality, she returned from her holiday still troubled and conflicted. Meanwhile, during her absence, Margaret had made it clear to Father Robert that, in the event of a total breakdown in relations, her loyalty would lie with her friend and not with him.

That August Margaret and Teresa agreed to join Father Robert and his two sons on a retreat to the island of Iona. They were to stay in the Bishop's House, an imposing, granite Gothic-style dwelling built in the late nineteenth century by the Lord Bishop of Argyll as a centre for prayer and contemplation, overlooking the Sound of Iona. Despite the beautiful surroundings and the atmosphere of deep peace, Teresa's inner turmoil continued, this time accompanied by severe headaches. One day, feeling totally overwhelmed, she retreated to her bed after dinner and looking across the Sound began to pray in desperation when suddenly, she recalled:

> I felt the entire load lifted from me, the pain in my head ceased as well as the turmoil in my soul. I saw clearly and without emotion, either of fear or joy, that I must tell Father Robert that we must go in the way Our Lord had showed me, whether he thought we were wrong or not.

She was aware that this would mean leaving Paisley and Father Robert's guidance, but was convinced that "all that mattered was that the path, however hard it might turn out to be, was clear and plain before me".

In typically fearless fashion, the next morning she went to confession and informed Father Robert of everything she had experienced. He declared flatly that she was entirely wrong and refused to discuss the matter any further until the penultimate day of their retreat. In the meantime, she discussed her experience in depth with Margaret, who was entirely supportive of her decision to leave. The two women finally met with Father Robert for what turned out to be a difficult and painful interview. It was agreed that they would stay in Paisley until the following spring to give him time to find replacements to carry out their parish work. Their only stipulation was Father Robert should not involve himself in their future plans and that he should not mention their proposed departure to the parishioners until nearer the time of their leaving.

The group headed back to Paisley at the beginning of September in sombre mood. After only a couple of weeks, Teresa's headaches returned, this time accompanied by vertigo. She was clearly in no fit state to work, so at the end of September the women decided to bring forward their leaving date. Margaret offered to pay for someone to carry out their duties until the following spring and then set about organizing their departure. Teresa was tasked with deciding where they should go. Although her thoughts had turned once more to Cornwall, she decided in the first instance she should visit Mother Ivy and Sister Rosanna to talk over their plans. The two elderly Sisters were now living in a small red-brick, semi-detached house, St Michael's, in Whitwell on the Isle of Wight, having left Duxford in 1915 for health reasons.[2]

Leaving Paisley was a miserable experience for Teresa, who was too ill to see many of the people of the parish with whom she had become close. On the day before her departure, she went to confession with Father Robert, but there was to be no final rapprochement. She recalled: "He was most stern, telling me what we were doing was not of God and we were quite mistaken!" With this warning ringing in her ears, she left for Whitwell, stopping off in London for a night on her journey. Here she met the female heart surgeon who had operated on her three years previously. Concerned for her friend's health, she insisted Teresa should see a heart specialist, who immediately diagnosed her with "a badly over-tired" heart and prescribed six months of rest, free from arduous work and responsibilities.

And so, in the same month she turned 40, without a job and suffering from chronic health issues, Teresa departed for the Isle of Wight. Reflecting on the two years in Paisley—despite the grim conditions, emotional conflict and frequent disapproval—she drew comfort from the deep bond of love and fellowship that had developed between her and Margaret. The reassurance this relationship gave her must have been a source of great strength as she turned her thoughts once again towards another new start.

Unknown to Teresa at this time, the Paisley years had a further significant legacy, which did not become apparent until many years later. Two of the girls she and Margaret had encountered in their work—a nursery school assistant and the daughter of the woman they had nursed with Bright's disease—had been so drawn to them and their way of life that they were later to join them in sisterhood.

Notes

[1] Paisley on the Web, "Church of the Holy Trinity and St Barnabas", <https://www.paisley.org.uk/paisley-history/church-holy-trinity-st-barnabas/>, accessed 5 July 2021.

[2] Whitwell History: Isle of Wight, "St Mary's House", <http://whitwellhistory.co.uk/history/>, accessed 12 May 2021.

CHAPTER 7

A pair of odd adventurers

Disregarding the six months of rest recommended by the London heart surgeon, Teresa allowed herself two weeks of recuperation with the elderly Sisters on the Isle of Wight. She spent this time researching locations and properties, before identifying a suitable cottage in St Agnes, Cornwall: a parish she thought would suit both her and Margaret as it had an Anglo-Catholic church.

Following her brief stay on the Isle of Wight, she joined Margaret at a small cottage in Sussex lent to them by the Franciscan Order of Elizabeth of Hungary. Here they set about the task of trying to re-create the religious dress Teresa had envisaged during her prayers at St Hilary. Eventually, "with much painful and puzzled effort", they produced habits of brown cloth with a large red cross on the scapular[*] and headdresses of starched white linen with distinctive winged sides.[†] Father Robert graciously assented to bless their new habits, which they sent him by post.

At the end of November 1928, the newly attired Sisters set off on the Cornish Riviera Express for their new home. Teresa, with her characteristic sense of the absurd, recollected the comedy of that first outing in their constricting outfits, as they tried to find handkerchiefs and negotiate their sandwich lunch. This feeling of self-consciousness continued after their arrival in the late afternoon at St Agnes, where they were aware of "a good many wondering and curious looks".

---

[*] Brown habits were traditionally worn by members of the Franciscan order and were later adopted by the FSJM.

[†] Similar in form to the cornette worn by the French Catholic order of the Daughters of Charity.

Teresa had been looking forward to returning to the mild climate and pastoral landscape of Cornwall, for which she had pined during her exile in Paisley. However, St Agnes, as a former industrial settlement, had a very different character to the rural parishes of St Hilary and Blisland. By the time the Sisters arrived, the last mine had closed, but the area's former industrial character, as Pevsner notes, was "still strikingly evoked by the thick scatter of abandoned chimneys and engine houses in the almost treeless landscape".[1]

As Teresa and Margaret were driven through the village by the station taxi driver, much to their consternation they did not stop in the centre with its assortment of public buildings, hotel and inns but continued some distance down a steep hill. At this point, they realized their new home was, contrary to the assurances of their landlord, nowhere near the church. On entering their new home, Perran Cot, they were further dismayed to find filthy floors, damp walls and a kitchen range that belched smoke into the kitchen.

The Sisters had arrived after nightfall, but the following morning they were delighted to find that their new cottage, despite its deficiencies, was close to the sea. They set about unblocking the chimney and removing years of grime from the linoleum floors, but no amount of scrubbing and clearing could counteract the bone-chilling damp of the neglected building. Even its picturesque location, above the former mineral harbour of Trevaunance Cove, had its downside, as it was situated a steep 20 minutes' walk from the church—far from ideal for Teresa with her heart condition. They persevered with the situation for five weeks, during which time Teresa began to suffer painful attacks of neuritis, before moving at the beginning of January 1929 to a new cottage, primitive but dry, closer to the church.

The Sisters had just begun to make friends among the congregation, having received a "pleasant and kind" reception from the vicar Father Browne, when their assimilation into life at St Agnes was abruptly suspended by the news on 9 January of the sudden death of Annie, Teresa's mother. Departing immediately for St Leonards-on-Sea, they arrived in time for Teresa to see her mother laid-out in her coffin. She movingly recalled the scene:

> She lay in an austere, serene beauty and peace which was beyond description. My Mother, who had known and suffered so many hard things, had retained almost to the end of her life a quality of child-like gaiety and simplicity which came out at the slightest provocation, whatever her troubles at that time might be.

The death of Annie had a profound effect on Teresa: on returning to Cornwall, she contracted pleurisy and was confined to bed for a fortnight. Margaret, anxious for her friend's wellbeing, found them more comfortable accommodation in the form of a pretty cottage with a sunny garden, close to the cliff path. She then proposed they spend the legacy of £100* she had recently been bequeathed on a pilgrimage.

They decided on Assisi, as they had not yet formally professed themselves as followers of a particular rule but were interested in learning more about the life of St Francis. This interest may have been influenced by previous encounters with Franciscans on Teresa's spiritual journey, including her conversion by the Franciscan friar, Father Andrew, and their recent stay with the Franciscan Sisters in Sussex.†

They left Cornwall in mid-April, beginning their pilgrimage in Florence and Siena. Teresa's description of these first few days is characteristic in its blend of spirituality and levity. She wrote movingly of Siena and "the tiny bare room in which Saint Catherine lived and prayed for three years, and where the human spirit of the girl Catherine is still pulsating", while also recounting a humorous episode where they spent the day unconsciously wearing each other's cloaks—Teresa's trailing on the ground and Margaret's comically short—until their mistake was pointed out to them by an amused shopkeeper.

In addition to learning more about the life of St Francis, the Sisters also hoped their act of pilgrimage would make it clear to them whether they should approach the Bishop of Truro to seek his blessing for their future plans. Their eight-day stay in the remarkable hillside town of

---

*   The equivalent of *c*.£6,000 today.

†   Another influence may have been the habits they had adopted which were made from brown cloth, a colour traditionally associated with Franciscan friars.

Assisi with its beautiful light, exquisite churches, plethora of shrines and soundtrack of peeling bells provided a wealth of meaningful experiences and encounters which helped to strengthen their resolve. Attending Mass on their first morning in the crypt of the Basilica of San Francesco where the bones of St Francis are kept, both Teresa and Margaret felt, despite the overcrowding, "a great and deep peace ... to each of us it spoke of the profound and serene peace of a perfect death", followed by an understanding "that the secret of St Francis, and his message to the world, is enshrined in the complete surrender to death of the natural man, in him, in order that his life be identified with the love and life of Christ".

On another occasion, they met a Roman Catholic priest in the sacristy of the basilica who observed: "You too have a share in St Francis, may you grow and prosper", before giving them his blessing. Visiting the small church of San Damiano, where St Francis had his vision of Christ on the crucifix asking him to rebuild His church, the Sisters were taken to a side chapel by a friar who pointed to the face of Christ on the cross with the words "after death, peace", an expression they felt charged with meaning following their experience in the basilica crypt. Less encouraging was the friar conducting a group of American tourists around St Mary of the Angels, the once-tiny chapel in the woods where St Francis began the Franciscan movement, which had been subsequently rebuilt as a grand church in the sixteenth century. On hearing they were Anglicans, the friar remarked: "Well you will never come to any good unless you are founded on the Rock of Peter." "Too bad, Sisters, to call you out like that", one of the Americans murmured.

An important item on their itinerary was to visit a group of women living a life following the teachings of St Francis in a hermitage on a hillside in Umbria. They had learnt about these women from a friend in Paisley, who may well have read an article in *The Spectator* written by the theologian and mystic Evelyn Underhill, who had visited the Italian Sisters at the Hermitage of Campello the previous year. Underhill had found the experience profoundly moving, noting:

> Certainly nothing has ever brought me so near to the real Franciscan spirit as a few hours spent in the Vale of Spoleto with a little group of women who are trying to bring back to modern

> existence the homely, deeply supernatural and quite un-monastic ideal of the Primitive Rule.[2]

She went on to describe how the Sisters lived as a small family, leading a life of prayer in the small chapel converted from a stable, working the poor mountain land, weaving cloth and giving hospitality to those who sought it.

The community had been founded by Sister (Sorella) Maria, who referred to herself as the Least Sister. A former Franciscan nun, she left her conventional order to follow more closely the life of St Francis. Sorella Maria's belief in ecumenism—"The Light can come from far away ... We are not the only ones who possess the Truth. From the sacred books of different peoples can come to us a ray of Light"[3]—had resulted in the women being ostracized by the Roman Catholic Church. However, despite this hostility from the Church authorities, the unconventional group of women, known locally as the Larks of St Francis, had developed an international reputation. Among the people with whom Sorella Maria was in correspondence were Mahatma Ghandi, Albert Schweitzer and the psychiatrist Roberto Assagiolli.

Finding the Larks turned out to be a significant act of pilgrimage. Teresa and Margaret hired a taxi to travel the 20 miles south from Assisi and then faced a 45-minute scramble up a mountainside. The beauty of their surroundings, however, more than made up for any physical discomfort. Teresa recalled:

> As we approached the Eremo the chapel bell was rung as a welcome to us, by one of the Sorellina. We loved the place, and the wonderful views over the Vale of Spoleto, and the solitary little olive wood above the house and chapel.

Unfortunately, they had not arrived at a good time—several of the Sisters were away, the only Sister who could speak English was ill and the founder, Sorella Maria, was also unwell.

After lunch in the refectory, they were taken to meet Sorella Jacopa, the second-in-command who was blind but could communicate with Margaret in French. Jacopa commented on the love she could perceive between Teresa and Margaret and observed "where there is union of hearts there is no barrier of race, or creed or colour"—echoing one of the tenets on which Sorella Maria had founded the order and which at that time put them out of communion with the Roman Catholic Church.

Then came the welcome news that Sorella Maria herself would like to see them. Despite the lack of a shared language, Sorella Maria kissed the cross on Teresa's habit and joined together her hands with those of Teresa and Margaret. Teresa regarded this as a significant act of affirmation, observing that by this act: "My own vision of our life and community was greatly strengthened."

They returned to Cornwall greatly heartened by the pilgrimage, and Teresa resolved to write to the Bishop of Truro, Walter Frere, requesting his support and blessing. Meanwhile the Sisters began to carry out social work in the parish which included helping the elderly, assisting a lady who had recently had her sixth child and collecting the pensions for four blind people who lived in the village. The vicar asked them to take on the work in the sacristy—helping to clean and prepare the vestments, linen and sacred vessels—and they began a weekly prayer group. In many respects, the Sisters' life in St Agnes had clear parallels with their time in Paisley except for one major difference; they now had the outward appearance of religious. However, this was to prove problematic as, despite the acceptance and support of the vicar, they had received no response to their request for support from the diocesan bishop. Their lack of official status prompted a prominent member of the congregation, whose sister was in one of the major religious orders, to refer to them as upstarts. Further hostility came from a group of religious Sisters in the parish who ran a convalescent home for men.[*]

Teresa and Margaret waited with increasing impatience for a reply from the bishop. They might have expected a positive response, as Bishop Frere was himself a religious, a member of the Community of the Resurrection, Mirfield.[4] Finally word came, but rather than writing directly to Teresa, the bishop wrote to their vicar, Father Browne, suggesting Teresa and Margaret should join another group of women he knew. He then wrote again to the vicar noting that they should not be

---

[*] A branch house of the Community of the Epiphany, Truro, founded in 1883.

referring to themselves as "Sisters". Father Browne passed on the letters to Teresa, who countered the suggestions "as respectfully but as firmly as possible". Eventually, in December, Bishop Frere informed Father Browne he was prepared to meet Teresa and Margaret when he came to St Agnes to preach at the patronal festival the following January. Father Browne, revealing his confidence in the Sisters' vocations, advised them to "begin as good obedient children ... but if he tries to deflect you tell him you believe God has called you and you must go on".

When the bishop eventually came, the Sisters found him "kind and fatherly". He spoke to them about Divine Vocation and prayed with them in the little oratory they had constructed in their cottage, after which he gave legitimacy to their status as religious by granting them permission to carry out village missioning.

On Whit Tuesday, June 1930, the Sisters set off on a three-week mission tour to three parishes recommended to them by the bishop. Their accommodation had been arranged in advance, but they decided, in the spirit of the mendicant friars, to travel without money. As part of their mission, they planned to hold open-air meetings with hymn singing accompanied by Sister Margaret on her piano accordion, named Jacapone after one of the followers of St Francis (it was tribute to Margaret's vocation that she was prepared to employ her highly developed musical skills on such a humble instrument). To raise their profile, they carried a banner, made for them by Mother Etheldred from the Order of St Anne, with whom Teresa had stayed in Boston. This gift indicated not only that the Sisters in the United States still held Teresa in their affections, but were also supportive of her efforts to pursue a life as a religious under her own terms.

The mission began well with the offer of a lift the 32 miles to their first destination of St Blazey from a member of their prayer group. The journey took a whole day and they arrived at St Blazey vicarage in time for supper with the vicar, Father Gendall. The Sisters then went to the houses allocated for their lodgings for the next ten days: Teresa with the local doctor and his sister, and Margaret with the village schoolmistress. The following evening, feeling nervous and apprehensive, they held their first open-air meeting, the sounds of the accordion and singing soon attracting a small crowd. Teresa recalled how the vicar had begun the proceedings:

"He was very glad he had come and glad to be at the meeting to speak, but did not suppose or expect any great good to come from it all but was glad we were there." After this somewhat underwhelming endorsement, the Sisters determined in future to dispense with an introduction from the parish priest.

St Blazey at the time of the Sisters' mission was a small industrial town. A former agricultural village, its expansion in the early nineteenth century in response to the local tin and copper industries was similar to that of St Agnes. St Blazey, however, was still an industrial settlement, with the processing and export of china clay replacing the former heavy metal enterprises.[5] Despite the thriving industry, Teresa and Margaret soon learnt from their hosts of the widespread deprivation in the town. Teresa later recalled:

> St Blazey was a bad little place, with a lot of very poor and slummy cottages, a great deal of illness mostly T.B. and (according to the doctor) much venereal disease and much immorality.

The Sisters experienced the poverty of St Blazey first hand when they went to visit a "horribly dirty" lodging house that was run by a woman who was practically blind, assisted by her inadequate daughter. Teresa described their visit:

> In one room a man kept chickens under his bed; in another an Irish sailor was in an unspeakably dirty bed coughing up his lungs in an advanced state of T.B. It took a great deal of courage to kneel and pray in this house, but the woman who kept the house, and the almost dying sailor, were pleased and grateful for our visit and for the prayers.

Equally memorable, but for more positive reasons, was their visit to a large commercial laundry which employed 70 girls and young women. After lengthy negotiations with the unenthusiastic manager, they were allowed 15 minutes to talk to the girls during their lunch hour. Teresa recalled: "We have always kept a pleasant memory of the girls in their pretty summer frocks sitting on tables and benches to listen to what we said." They continued each evening to hold their open-air meetings and during the day visited the school, Mothers' Union meetings and made house calls. Teresa noted they were most happily received in the poorer houses but found the more comfortably off not so forthcoming.

They set out for their second village, St Mewan, feeling far more confident in their endeavour, with their bus fares paid for by donations received in St Blazey. This time they stayed with the vicar and his wife in their sizeable vicarage but saw little of their hosts except on Sunday. Here the open-air meetings were easier to conduct, as there was a village green, and they were pleased to draw groups of between 40 and 50 people. Their greatest supporters were a group of older Methodist women whose manner impressed Teresa: "They were of those who really know and love God, and walk with him as friends."

By the time they reached their final destination, the churchtown of St Stephen-in-Brannel to the west of St Austell, the Sisters' growing confidence and the welcome support of the vicar, Father Gilbert, ensured this mission was their most successful. Not only did Father Gilbert offer Teresa and Margaret accommodation at the vicarage he shared with his two sisters, but he had also prepared lists of the local roads annotated with the names of the church attenders who lived there. Visiting sometimes singly and sometimes together, one morning the Sisters were surprised to be received into a cottage by a woman, who without a word led them upstairs. As she opened the bedroom door, they were confronted by a coffin in which lay the dead body of her husband.

The Sisters greatly admired the local church, a fifteenth-century granite structure given a High Church restoration in the late nineteenth century by the West Country architect G. H. Fellowes Prynne. They were also very pleased with the village hall where they held Sunday evening mission services in addition to their well-attended open-air meetings. As in the previous parishes, their mission continued to have ecumenical appeal, this time with members of the Salvation Army.

Heartened by the success of the mission, they resolved, on their return to St Agnes at the end of June, to approach Bishop Frere with a request to make their first vows. As far as they were concerned, they had entered the condition of novices in September 1926 when they began their work in Paisley, and consequently it was now time to take the next step in their religious journey. Unfortunately for the Sisters, the Bishop of Truro was ill, having recently suffered a stroke, and their own vicar, Father Browne, was also unwell. It is indicative of their determination to progress in religious life that, rather than waiting for either of the men to regain his health, they approached the assistant priest who was helping out at St Agnes, to hear their vows.* Before this took place, however, they decided to go on retreat for a few days.

Teresa chose the enclosed order of the Society of the Precious Blood (SPB) at Burnham Abbey for their retreat. This decision turned out to be most fortuitous, as the SPB was a relatively new order and its founder, Mother Millicent Mary, was most supportive of the Sisters' desire to form their own community. There was much in the formation of the SPB which mirrored the recent experiences of Teresa and Margaret and would anticipate some of what was to come. Mother Millicent, born Millicent Taylor, the daughter of an army officer, founded the community in 1905 in an inner-city parish in Birmingham. The Sisters' involvement in parish visiting, teaching at the Sunday school and running a club for factory girls was very similar to the work carried out by Teresa and her Sisters in Paisley. Over time, the SPB developed and moved, first to follow a stricter life of prayer at a former farmhouse in King's Heath, to the south of Birmingham, then to Hendon, before finally, as the community grew and Mother Millicent felt increasingly drawn to the contemplative life, to Burnham Abbey, where they purchased the recently restored former Augustinian abbey.[6]

Her experiences in founding the SPB aroused Mother Millicent's sympathies with regard to the opposition the Sisters had faced. Teresa later recalled: "She knew how hateful communities could be to those just beginning", before reflecting: "We were then, and always have been, most grateful for the way the Society of the Precious Blood welcomed

---

* Bishop Frere recovered from his stroke and continued as Bishop of Truro until 1935, when he returned to the Community of the Resurrection, Mirfield, the order he had co-founded. He died three years later in 1938. Father William Browne recovered from his illness and continued as vicar of St Agnes until his death in 1933. He is buried in St Agnes churchyard.

us when we were just a pair of odd adventurers with no ecclesiastical backing or approval."

After three happy days in the delightful surroundings of the thirteenth-century abbey, they returned to St Agnes and made their first vows on 16 July 1930 before the assistant priest. During the ceremony, they took off their black belts and replaced them with white Franciscan cords, which had been blessed at the altar.* The Sisters settled down to a calm and productive period: their lives occupied by domestic duties, sacristy work, visiting the sick and the weekly prayer group. This tranquil period, however, proved to be short-lived, as before long they found themselves the central players in a local controversy.

It began with a cry for help from a young woman, Phyl, who had recently been diagnosed with diphtheria. Her doctor had advised she be nursed at home or go to the local isolation hospital. As Phyl's mother was a semi-invalid and they could not afford the hospital, the Sisters agreed that she and her mother should come to stay with them in their cottage. The arrangement was approved by the village doctor, who gave the Sisters detailed instructions on infection control which they carried out scrupulously. They had not anticipated, however, the reaction in St Agnes. Teresa recalled:

> The whole village went off the deep end about us having the girl in the house, and I came home to find a note from the Vicar in which he said that God would reward and bless us for our charity but that we mustn't go to Mass or indeed to church at all because the faithful were very upset and worried about the fear of getting diphtheria.

The reaction of the villagers was understandable; diphtheria was a highly infectious disease with a one-in-ten chance of death for those who came into contact with it. At this point, vaccination had not been introduced in the UK and every year the illness killed on average 3,500 children.[7] The

---

* The white cord with three knots representing poverty, chastity and obedience was later adopted by the FSJM. "Cord" was the term used by the Sisters, but it is also known as a cincture or a girdle.

Sisters, however, confident they were following all the correct medical guidance, did not accept that they should not be allowed to receive Holy Communion. They believed that "the Sacrament would preserve our bodies as well as our souls" and made it clear to the vicar they would present themselves at the end of Mass each day to receive the Sacrament. This arrangement was accepted by the vicar and followed by the Sisters for the next six weeks throughout the duration of Phyl's illness.

Looking back on the incident, Teresa recalled a "state of siege", where they could not visit the shops and no one would come near them apart from their Nonconformist neighbour who did their shopping. She was unimpressed by what she saw as a lack of faith among her fellow churchgoers and remarked wryly how, after Phyl had recovered and no one else in the village contracted diphtheria, "the tide turned in our favour and the foolish village and church people begun to say how wonderful the Brown Sisters were".

This raising of the Sisters' profile reignited the tensions with the Community of the Epiphany who ran the village convalescent home. The Mother Superior contacted Father Browne, saying she intended to withdraw her Sister who was assisting with the Sunday school, as he clearly had no need of her. Teresa and Margaret felt the consequences of this action could place them in an invidious position and began to contemplate a move. Their minds were made up when a further health issue for Teresa, this time deafness in one ear, required her to make frequent visits to a specialist in London. And so, in September 1931, they made the decision once again to leave Cornwall.

Notes

[1] Beacham and Pevsner, *Cornwall*, p. 488.
[2] Evelyn Underhill, "A Franciscan Hermitage", *The Spectator* (11 February 1928), <http://archive.spectator.co.uk/article/11th-february-1928/7/a-franciscan-hermitage>, accessed 11 July 2018.
[3] Catherine Ann Lombard, "A Wild and Free Creature", *Love and Will*, <https://loveandwill.com/2018/06/05/a-wild-and-free-creature/#more-3078>, accessed 12 November 2021.

4   H. Miles Brown, *The Church in Cornwall* (Truro: Oscar Blackford Ltd, 1964), p. 110.
5   "Cornwall Industrial Settlements Initiative, St Blazey (with St Blazey Gate and West Par)", Historic Environment Service, Cornwall County Council, June 1999, accessed 12 December 2021.
6   "The Society of the Precious Blood (Burnham Abbey): an Anglican Contemplative Community", <http://www.burnhamabbey.org/history.htm>, accessed 16 January 2022.
7   "Diphtheria", *Vaccine Knowledge: University of Oxford*, accessed 24 January 2022.

CHAPTER 8

The road to London

The Sisters' search for somewhere nearer to London took them to the village of Hinton Martell in Dorset. A previous incumbent, Father Alban Baverstock, a prolific author and hymn writer, had made the church famous in Anglo-Catholic circles. The tiny village's other claim to fame was its somewhat incongruous fountain described in the 1906 *Highways and Byways of Dorset*:

> Hinton Martell, an out-of-the-world hamlet of thatched cottages, has a possession which is, so far as I know, unique among the attractions of hamlets. In what may be called the street is a circular basin, in the centre of which is just such a fountain as may be found in a suburban tea-garden or in front of a gaudy Italian villa... How this café chantant ornament has found its way into a modest and secluded hamlet there is no evidence to show.

By the time Teresa and Sister Margaret arrived in September 1931, the sleepy, back-of-beyond character of Hinton Martell still persisted, with the neighbouring Earl and Countess of Shaftesbury affording an almost feudal level of deference. The Sisters rented a small bungalow from the rector, Father David Taylor, with whom they became great friends. Unlike in Cornwall, where their religious dress had prompted a degree of hostility, in the more genteel atmosphere of Hinton Martell it was their behaviour which excited comment. Teresa recalled:

> The adult villagers looked on us at first with great suspicion, they decided among themselves almost at once that "The Sisters

were not ladies" because they saw us with sleeves rolled up and aprons on while we cleaned our bungalow and did our washing.

Nevertheless, they soon settled in, their principal activity being the reinstatement of the Sunday school. Before long all 26 of the village children became regular attenders and the villagers expressed their appreciation with gifts of vegetables, fruit and eggs left on their doorstep. By the time they staged an open-air *Pageant of Saints*, performed by the children, any lingering reservations about them had disappeared.

Beneath the surface, however, all was not well in this seemingly idyllic parish. Father Taylor began to confide in them his feelings of loneliness and unhappiness.[*] Teresa then faced her own personal crisis when she learnt that her stepfather, William Parsons, was close to death. Putting aside all feelings of past rejection, she went with Margaret to nurse him through the final difficult three weeks of his life. Parsons' attitude to Teresa had mellowed over the years since her mother died, and for her part, she had been working on forgiving him all the years since her first confession with Father Andrew. She later recalled her final conversation with her stepfather and the gratitude she felt to Father Andrew for enabling it to take place:

> He said 'Grace, don't leave me, I don't mind anything as long as you stay with me'. I suddenly saw myself saying 'I can't and I won't'.

What happened on their return to Hinton Martell is one of the strangest incidents ever recounted by Teresa and can only perhaps be understood in the context of the emotionally complex three weeks she had just endured. In her memoir, she wrote without further explanation:

> The Arch-enemy paid us some unwelcome and rather disturbing attention which had to be quelled by a thorough-going exorcism of both the exterior and interior of the bungalow.

---

[*] He was later to join the Catholic Church, becoming an Oratorian at the Brompton Oratory.

As the year progressed, the Sisters became increasingly more concerned about their troubled rector, fearing Father Taylor could leave at any moment. In addition, the work with the village children, while rewarding, was far from demanding. They felt a growing sense that they should go somewhere more in need of their services. Sister Margaret was keen to pursue a life of parish work of the type she had originally envisaged when taking on the flat in Paisley. Teresa later admitted:

> I was never keen on it, but she was and I thought it was fair on her that we should have a good go at proper parish work, so she could decide what she really felt about it.

They agreed that London was the most obvious choice for this venture with Teresa seeking the advice of her friend the woman surgeon. Her first suggestion, a parish in Camberwell, proved unsuitable, but the priest there recommended they try Father Langdon, the incumbent at St Matthew's Church, City Road.

On arriving at their destination, Teresa and Sister Margaret decided to look round the church before their appointment with the vicar. In 1848, the newly built St Matthew's had been celebrated in an article in the *Illustrated London News*:

> Very pleasing architectural character, its lofty tower and spire, in particular deserving great commendation ... Great praise must be awarded to the architect, Mr Scott, for this addition to the modern ecclesiastical edifices of London.[1]

The article was illustrated with a drawing featuring the magnificent tower and spire, which exhibited a marked similarity to the tower and spire of the Nikolaikirche in Hamburg, designed by George Gilbert Scott three years previously.[*] The *Illustrated London News* article continued to describe the consecration of St Matthew's, noting "the interior of the church is very elegant" and that the service was attended by "The Lord

---

[*] Ironically, the magnificent landmark qualities of both these structures caused them to be bombed during the Second World War.

Bishop of London, in the presence of a numerous and highly respectable congregation." Eighty-four years after its consecration, the contrast with this civilized and elegant scene could not have been more marked. Teresa recalled:

> Never will either of us forget our first look at it. The whole interior seemed to be almost dark full of cobwebs and gloom, and at the back of the church when we saw him which wasn't for a few minutes because he was crouching in a pew, was a man who said he was a police officer on watch because several little girls had been taken into the church by men and assaulted there.

The Sisters could have been forgiven if, at this point, they decided to return to Dorset and rethink their future plans, but undaunted they duly called on Father Langdon. His vicarage stood opposite the church, part of the once-elegant Oakley Crescent—a collection of tall buildings in London stock brick, the ecclesiastically appropriate Gothic vicarage contrasting with the elegant classical features of the neighbouring townhouses. During this first meeting, the Sisters agreed to assist the vicar in his parish work and to move into the flat on the top floor of the vicarage, for which they would pay rent of £1.5.0 per week not including electricity.

They made the decision to go ahead with this plan despite a far from encouraging initial meeting. Teresa later recalled: "He was a sad priest for he told us any love for souls he had ever had was gone a long time ago. It all looked rather discouraging, the church the Vicar and the neighbourhood." Describing their time in City Road, she made few further references to Father Langdon, other than to confirm this first impression of a man disillusioned and ineffectual.* In his heyday, Father

---

* This had not always been the case. The Revd Charles Godfrey Langdon was Cambridge-educated and, prior to taking on the benefice of St Matthew's, City Road in 1928, had made a name for himself as the vicar of St Michael's, Poplar, which at that time (1913–28) was one of the poorest parishes in London. Father Langdon, a Labour supporter and social reformer, supported the Poplar Rates Rebellion in 1921, and his tireless commitment to the

Langdon's social and political leanings, similar to those of Bernard Walke, would have greatly appealed to the Sisters, but sadly by the time they met he was burnt out. No longer functioning effectively as a cleric, he had re-directed his energies into a successful parallel career as a silversmith, producing highly regarded domestic and ecclesiastical silverware in the Arts and Crafts style.[2]

On moving to the City Road in September 1932, the Sisters' main task, as in their former parish in Dorset, was to run the Sunday school. This was set up in one of the two main rooms of their flat, using Teresa's small inheritance from her stepfather to buy the necessary equipment. Each day they recited the office in an oratory formed from a boxroom and visited the church to pray in the chapel where the Blessed Sacrament was reserved—this being the best kept space in the neglected church.

After a period of settling in, they began parish visiting. The area had changed radically over the years: the former, prosperous villa owners had moved out into the newly developed suburbs, leaving behind houses now subdivided into multiple occupancy dwellings. These were now home to an ever-growing population employed in the warehouses, factories and works which had sprung up around the Regent's Canal.[3] Teresa recalled:

> Fifty years before it had been a well-to-do neighbourhood, but it had deteriorated into an area where all the houses, mostly of eleven rooms, were housing three or four families ... our neighbourhood was a poor one and we found many families in need. The majority of them lived in two rooms, however large their families, only a minority had a house or flat to themselves.

The first few months proved a struggle, not helped by Sister Margaret contracting mumps. However, 1933 started positively with the arrival of their first postulant, a young woman, Dorothy Bee, who moved into

---

deprived people of his parish was recognized posthumously when Langdon Park was named after him in the 1950s. Despite being a pacifist, Langdon served as an army chaplain in the First World War and was a supporter of women's higher education, his own daughter Mollie becoming a doctor who practised in the Poplar area.

their cramped quarters in the vicarage flat, sleeping in a camp bed in the playroom. She enthusiastically embraced the Sunday school work and encouraged two of her friends, Mary Fletcher and May Woodrow, to help.[*]

Teresa described the nascent community at this time as "a rather unusual little group of women with no ecclesiastical authority or backing, except that when I had a brief interview with the Bishop of London [Bishop Arthur Winnington-Ingram] on our arrival in London he had given us his blessing." However, despite their somewhat unorthodox character, the Sisters received clerical support from Father Robert Gofton Salmond, a young vicar in the neighbouring parish of St Clement's, Lever Street, which ministered to some of the most deprived in a poor area. He agreed to hear the Sisters' confessions and lent his support to their community when he was able.

During the summer of 1933, Dorothy Bee was clothed as a novice, taking the religious name Sister Clare. The vicarage flat, now housing three women and an ever-increasing Sunday school, was no longer suitable for their purposes. Just as they were looking round for suitable accommodation, the house next door came on the market. Much altered over the years, the 11-roomed house had been extended at the rear to include a workshop from which the current owner, Signor Quintillio Dini, had run a hat blocking business, renting the remaining rooms to four families. Due to its dilapidated condition, and only ten years remaining on the lease, he agreed to sell the property for £500.[†] This was a considerable sum of money, and it is illustrative of the Sisters' ambition that they even considered taking on such a large property at this stage in the development of the community.

It is unclear how they had been supporting themselves up to this point. Teresa had no financial reserves, but Sister Margaret most likely had a small income[‡]—possibly from her own family or inherited from

---

[*] May Woodrow was to later become an Extern Sister of the FSJM.

[†] Equivalent to c.£46,000 today.

[‡] We know Margaret had been planning to live by herself in the tenement in Paisley before she was joined by Teresa, Jean and Emma, suggesting she had the means to finance this scheme.

her late husband. We do know, however, that it was from Margaret that the funds came to purchase the lease of the house on Oakley Crescent. Margaret's brother, Dr George Buckley, who was living with their mother in a house bequeathed to Margaret when her mother died, agreed to advance Margaret £600 on the future sale of the house. This enabled the Sisters not only to take on the lease, but to install electric light, a hot water system and a bath. Other essential works of renovation and refurbishment took place with the help of young people from the church, including the conversion of the workshop into a space for missions and the Sunday school and the modification of the rear portion of the main ground-floor room, divided from the sitting room by a set of doors, into an oratory. Teresa recalled what an important oasis of calm this space became: "For the sounds of wireless sets in the tightly packed houses behind ours assailed our ears especially in the evening."

Ever mindful of the need to legitimize their status, Teresa contacted the local bishop, Charles Curzon, the Bishop of Stepney, and asked him if he would come one Sunday to bless their house and talk to the Sunday school. The bishop duly agreed and, to emphasize the significance of the occasion, a set of three black and white photographs was commissioned from a local photographer to record the event. One shows a typical Anglo-Catholic procession leaving the house: a thurifer and boat boys, followed by the crucifer, the three Sisters, more servers carrying lights in weighty candlesticks and, just emerging from the front door, Bishop Curzon in his robes and mitre wearing his distinctive round glasses and gentle smile. Either side of the entrance stand members of the Sunday school, some carefully restrained by their watchful mothers. In a second, the procession moves around the church, its route marked by a double row of children, this time older and with few attendant mothers. Everyone is clearly wearing their Sunday best, with the boys in shorts and jackets, many of the girls in berets and all the mothers in hats. In the third, the procession has finally reached the southern side of the church, but whatever ceremony is being performed by the bishop is obscured by a further crowd of children.

Recalling the day of the house blessing, Teresa observed:

> We had a grand Sunday afternoon with the children and the young people who during the first year had become our friends ... The few adults who belonged to the church, alas, were very unresponsive. They did not like us or our new ways of doing things and evidently felt that we were usurping their places.

Soon after the ceremony, another young woman, Rose Terry, who wished to test her vocation, joined the Sisters for a brief period. She was a machinist in one of the local factories producing cheap silk dresses and underwear and was known locally for her good behaviour and piety. She persevered for a while but was ultimately discouraged from taking her vocation further, as Teresa was not convinced Rose was suited to the life—the episode illustrative of Teresa's sincere intentions to build a legitimate community.

The Sisters threw themselves into their work with varying degrees of success. The Sunday school was a triumph. Conscious of the deprivation in which the children lived, the Sisters were determined to provide them with good quality toys and books to play with, paid for by Sister Margaret's brother. On dry days in the summer, the Sunday school took place on the large area of grass bordered by railings to the south of the church and proved very popular with the young people. Teresa later recalled they had 300 children on their books for Sunday school, with an average attendance of 276.

In addition to maintaining the large house and running the Sunday school, they revived the open-air mission work with banner and accordion, held film and slide evenings in their recently repurposed mission room and encouraged the parishioners to take part in an Easter Vigil in the church. Teresa recalled these endeavours with her typical pragmatism and wry amusement: the open-air missions were abandoned, as "it was not a very certain good"; the slideshows frequently took place with the Sisters holding an umbrella over the equipment as the roof leaked and during the vigil the children came first "to pray, and then to be a nuisance".

In October 1934, they were joined by the postulant Doris Kathleen Coysh, who took the religious name of Sister Bernadine. She was 33 years old and, like Sister Margaret, a widow.* Also like Sister Margaret she had shared a talent with her late husband whom she had met through their work as draughtsmen.[4] Sister Bernadine's arrival was most fortuitous, as it coincided with a period of ill health for Teresa. This began with a severe carbuncle on the back of her neck (an indication she was run-down) and progressed to another heart episode. Teresa consequently recognized the need to scale-back some of her ambitions: the mission services on Sunday evening were dropped.

In March 1935, Sister Bernadine received the habit. This occasion prompted both Teresa and Margaret to think about their own religious journey and to consider the possibility of their taking life vows. This was to prove far from straightforward. Father Salmond, who had become the Sisters' warden in 1934, agreed to approach the Bishop of London, via Bishop Curzon, on their behalf. Their request was met with a couple of searching questions from the Bishop of London: "Were the Sisters serving the Church in a way that was not already done by an existing Religious Community?" and "What was the state of their finances?" The Sisters' response did not satisfy the bishop and his decision not to sanction the Sisters' life professions was conveyed to them via a regretful Bishop Curzon. While making it clear that he could not defy his diocesan bishop's authority by carrying out the service himself, Bishop Curzon indicated he would not have a problem with Father Salmond receiving the Sisters' vows.

Accordingly, the Sisters began to plan for their profession, which was due to take place in June at St Clement's, Father Salmond's church. Unexpectedly they heard the Bishop of London had performed a volte face and had written to the Bishop of Stepney saying he was happy for him to receive the Sisters' vows on his behalf. The reason for this change of heart is not known—it could have been in response to lobbying from some of the Sisters' well-connected supporters or the bishop's pragmatic desire that, if the ceremony were to take place, it should do so in accordance with correct procedure. Bishop Curzon stipulated the service should take place in their parish church of St Matthew's, much to the chagrin of Father Langdon.

---

* They were both possibly war widows.

Teresa set about making arrangements for the ceremony with her characteristic enthusiasm and a certain degree of mischief. The church was given a thorough spring clean and invitations sent to all the local women who had become their friends through fundraising events and support for the Sunday school—so far so conventional. More surprising, however, was the sport Teresa decided to have with the convention of the ceremony of the profession of vows being referred to as a wedding ceremony. Having received money from a friend to buy a cake for the post-service reception, Teresa set off for Selfridges: "The young woman who received my request for a two-tiered cake with a bordering of sugar roses in red and white and two white hearts on the top with the name Teresa in red on one heart and Margaret on the other, looked at me with cold incredulity and said 'Are you sure that is what you want?'" Amused by this reaction, Teresa then set off to order a bouquet for Margaret of pink sweet peas and white daisies. She recalled: "Asked by the assistant 'Excuse me, Madam, but is this sheaf to be for a presentation or a funeral?' 'Neither', said I gaily, 'it's for a wedding!' and the young woman almost collapsed with surprise."

This episode speaks volumes of the boldness, even recklessness, of Teresa's spirit; she was prepared to take the risk of reports of her behaviour getting back to the Bishop of London, knowing he had been reluctant to accept them in their role as independent religious. History does not record how those who attended the ceremony on 27 June 1935 responded to the cake. Teresa later recalled: "We had a small tea party on the Profession Day, but the real wedding party was on the following Monday evening when about forty of the women of the neighbourhood came." This gathering of a large number of mainly working-class women, some of whom suffered extreme poverty, recalls the Sisters' previous moving episode with the women at the Cornish laundry.

Despite the unorthodox celebrations, there is little doubt Teresa and Sister Margaret took the act of their profession with the utmost solemnity. Both had been on retreat prior to the ceremony, with Teresa returning to the community at Duxford and Sister Margaret to the Community of the Holy Cross in Haywards Heath. Their own community now consisted of the two Sisters in life vows, the novices Bernadine and Clare, and a young woman, Eva Fennell, who was waiting to become a postulant. Just at this point, when the community seemed to be taking shape, Teresa suffered another heart attack, less than three weeks after receiving her life vows. Despite bed rest followed by a holiday on the Isle of Wight with Sister Margaret, Teresa struggled to recuperate and by October suffered a further attack, which kept her in bed for nearly a month. Finally, after consulting the heart specialist she had seen seven years previously, Teresa was advised she would never make a full recovery but could avoid further incidents if she led the life of a semi-invalid.

Despite her natural wilfulness, Teresa initially complied with the doctor's instructions, but found the whole experience immensely challenging: "It was all very hard and the mental and moral struggle to get stronger and bear with the weariness and loss of interest in things which I ought to care about, was a heavy burden, and I often found myself wishing that I could give up the effort of living altogether." Eventually this painful period of poor physical health and its attendant acedia came to an end and to everyone's surprise she began to make a significant recovery.

Meanwhile, life in the small community had continued to evolve. Eva Fennell had been given the habit and taken the name Sister Christina, and an older woman Sister Margaret had befriended while on holiday in Weston-super-Mare was clothed and took the name Sister Agnes. Sister Clare made her temporary vows and, as a sign of her developing role within the community, joined Teresa and Sister Margaret on a large-scale mission at Mortlake Parish Church in 1936.

The community appeared to be finally back on track, but in early 1937 there was a further series of setbacks: Sister Christina was hospitalized with TB, Sister Clare began to consider an alternative vocation in mission work, and Sister Agnes concluded she was not happy in her new life and wished to leave. Teresa did her best to persuade Sister Agnes to reconsider her decision but to no avail, concluding with regret: "For some reason God was deliberately cutting us down."

In addition to the issue of recruiting and retaining members, the perennial problem of Teresa's relationship with clerical authority returned. Relations with their parish priest, which had begun tepid, were by this point distinctly frosty. Teresa recalled that, during the height of her heart episode when she was confined to bed, Father Langdon had reluctantly brought her sick communion, and each time this happened her blood pressure dropped alarmingly. In contrast, throughout her illness, her relationship with their warden, Father Salmond, remained good. Unfortunately, by early 1937 this was to change.

Teresa's recollection of the breakdown in their relations places the blame firmly at the door of Father Salmond: "We began to meet with difficulties with our Warden who was heading for a nervous breakdown, although no-one knew this at the time."

These "difficulties" centred around Father Salmond's desire for the Sisters to continue with their parish work, something Teresa felt was no longer possible given their depleted numbers. The situation had clear parallels with their latter years at Paisley, when Teresa was unwilling to accept Father Robert's insistence that parish work was more important than developing the community. Father Salmond, suffering with his mental health,* may well have acted with a lack of empathy towards the Sisters, but it is notable how, when recalling clerical opposition, Teresa felt the need to highlight the failings of the priest concerned rather than accept any responsibility for the situation herself. In the past, she had blamed Bernard Walke's ill health, Father Robert's almost bullying intransigence, the disquietude of Father Taylor and the disillusionment of Father Langdon. With no prospect of a mutually acceptable compromise, Father Salmond took the decision to stand down as their warden.

Despite this unsettling situation, some positive developments for the community took place that spring. Sister Bernadine made her first vows in March 1937, and a few months later they were joined by a young woman from South Africa, Constance Welfare. Sister Faith, as she was to become known, had suffered a double tragedy, losing her husband and then her daughter. Despite this new addition, by the end of July 1937, the Sisters had relinquished all their parish duties. Teresa recalled: "We had a growing conviction that parish work as we had been doing it in City Road was not really the work to which we were called by God."

Teresa became convinced that the community should seek a new home in the countryside and a visit to St Mary's, Whitwell in August

---

* Whatever personal issues Father Salmond may have been experiencing in 1937, his mental health was robust enough by 1953 to found his own religious order, the Community of the Servants of the Will of God.

persuaded her further when she saw that a house she had always admired was for let. Whitwell was familiar to Teresa and Sister Margaret through their visits to Mother Ivy and Sister Rosanna, and the local church had a style of worship they found agreeably high. Despite the complication of selling the lease on their house in London, they negotiated the rental of the house in Whitwell and forged ahead with their plans, not knowing until the day of their departure on 5 October that the sale had gone through.

The five years in London had seen many developments for the nascent order: five Sisters had joined and three had left; they had bought and sold their first community building; several hundred underprivileged children had been given a safe space to play in and a religious education; and they had made an important lifelong friend in Bishop Curzon. All this had been achieved despite their leader's chronic health problems. The chance to start again in an environment more congenial to Teresa's health must have given the four remaining Sisters cause for optimism.

Notes

[1] "St Matthew's Church, City Road", *Illustrated London News*, 15 April 1848.
[2] C. Langdon, "Charles Godfrey Langdon", *The Finial*, May/June 2009, <https://www.bexfield.co.uk/thefinial/pdf/19-05.pdf>, p. 17.
[3] "St Clement Finsbury: History", <https://www.stclementfinsbury.org/history.html>, accessed 14 February 2022.
[4] Information from correspondence with Mother Mary Agnes.

CHAPTER 9

An island interlude

As the home of the anchoresses Mother Ivy and Sister Rosanna, Whitwell on the Isle of Wight held particular significance for Teresa and her Sisters. The anchoresses were highly regarded, their vocations having been blessed by the Bishop of London.[1] Furthermore, Mother Ivy had a national reputation as head of a lay order of contemplatives known as the Order of the Holy Dove, which counted among its number Evelyn Underhill, the well-known spiritual writer and retreat leader.[2]

The anchoresses would undoubtedly have helped in the assimilation of the small community from London, alleviating some of the suspicion and animosity they had previously encountered in the rural communities of Cornwall and Dorset. Since their arrival in 1915, despite following a strict rule of silence and prayer, the figures of Mother Ivy and Sister Rosanna, clad in black habits and hoods, had become a familiar sight in the village. They lived in the heart of the community in a small semi-detached, red-brick house known as St Michael's and each year led confirmation classes for the local children. Consequently, the arrival of another small group of religious would have seemed less incongruous than in other rural settlements.

Teresa and her Sisters called their new home St Francis in honour of their patron saint. It was a sizeable house, dating from the 1750s, situated within a large garden, conveniently close to the church. Over the years, the original modest cottage had sprouted a collection of wings and accretions with a jumble of slate roofs; the whole leant charm by dove-grey freestone walls with contrasting fresh white paintwork and a veranda.

From their earlier visits to Whitwell, Teresa and Sister Margaret already had a passing acquaintance with a number of people in the village.

They were anxious, however, to get to know them better, along with the new young vicar and his wife. They had enjoyed good relations with the previous rector, an Anglo-Catholic, during whose incumbency the church had become a well-known centre for Catholic worship, with Mass said daily. To this end, shortly after their arrival, they decided to hold a house-warming party at St Francis which spilled out into the garden, allowing their guests to enjoy its autumnal beauty. The Sisters considered the event a great success, but a fortnight later, when Teresa called on the vicar with the intention of proposing a Christmas party for the village children, she found the vicar's response to her request astonishing: "To my surprise and horror the Vicar fell upon me with abuse and began to say every sort of unpleasant thing about us. He criticized our tea-party, saying it was extravagant, our garden, our clothes, everything in fact that he had seen of us."

As the uncomfortable interview progressed, it became clear the vicar was aggrieved by the Sisters' decision to go elsewhere for confession and ended by forbidding them from carrying out any parish duties. Unsurprisingly this incident resulted in Teresa suffering a heart episode and having to take to her bed for a number of days, after which the Sisters concluded their only course of action was to carry on with their own life within their community and let the dust settle.

The new year brought a letter from the vicar stating he intended to write to the Bishop of Portsmouth confirming his decision that the Sisters should not be allowed to do any work in the parish. It is unclear whether he carried out this threat, but shortly afterwards the Sisters received a letter from the bishop, Frank Partridge (who had previously welcomed them to his diocese), stating his intention of coming to bless their house, with the vicar acting as his chaplain. Teresa replied saying that she could not see how this could happen given the vicar's views. The bishop, living up to his description in *The Times* that year as "a man of wise counsel and clear vision",[3] declared his intention to visit Whitwell in order to get to the bottom of the matter. Teresa recalled: "It was all difficult and sad, for the Vicar's tale was mostly the gossip retold to him by one or two villagers who watched every tradesman and other persons who came to our house." Bishop Partridge admonished the vicar for his lack of charity, and the blessing of St Francis duly took place in May 1938 with the bishop assisted by ten priests. There was, however, no ensuing rapprochement between the vicar and the Sisters, the only continuing contact being in church.

Shortly before the contretemps over the house blessing, a significant event had taken place in the history of the community; in December 1937 they produced their first newsletter, *The Cord of St Francis*. The intention of the quarterly newsletter was to maintain a connection with the growing number of people, known as Externs, who had affiliated themselves to the community while maintaining their secular lives.[*] At this point, there were 26 Externs, including three groups in London, Birmingham and West Bromwich, Miss Betty Shaw in Paisley[†] and Gladys Hillier in Bridgwater.[‡] The first newsletter featured the motto of the community, *Nihil Amanti Impossibile*—"To love, nothing is impossible"—news of an upcoming retreat at Whitwell during Whitsuntide and a number of prayers. There was also a sentimental poem in the style of Longfellow's *Song of Hiawatha*, written under the pseudonym Sister Juniper. It opens with "Once a Mother and her daughters/Dwelt in London, London gloomy" and goes on to include the lines "Toil for those that God sent to them/Little thanks did there reward them", then later "Great the grief and deep the sorrow/Of their many friends in London ... Stretched out pleading hands to hold them/'Mother! Mother do not leave us'...", and so forth. Teresa could at times, occasionally in her memoir (but never subsequently in the newsletters), be defensive and exculpatory, but this was the sole instance of her countenancing a descent into mawkishness.

The lack of co-operation from the vicar meant the Sisters did not initially become as involved in parish life as they might have wished. However, support at diocesan level encouraged them to continue with the development of their community and to become involved in the wider religious life of the island. They began to speak at Mothers' Union meetings and were joined by two more women who wished to try their

---

[*] In conventional Franciscan communities this group of people are known as tertiaries.

[†] The nursery school assistant who had come to know the Sisters when they lived in Paisley and who would later join the FSJM as Sister Elizabeth.

[‡] Possibly Sister Margaret's friend who had tried her vocation in City Road.

vocations—Maud Robinson, one of the London Extern Sisters, and Dorothy Poole from Milton Abbey.* There were plenty of developments to report in the June 1938 newsletter: the success of their first retreat; news of a third woman, Morwenna Tredinnick, coming to test her vocation; and the official name the Sisters had chosen for their community—The Franciscan Servants of Jesus and Mary (FSJM).

The hostility of their vicar, initially such a devastating blow to the Sisters, had the positive outcome of prompting them to pursue a more wide-ranging mission than might have been the case had they taken an active role in parish life at Whitwell. The vicar of the nearby village of Godshill invited Sisters Bernadine and Margaret to run his Sunday school and a fortnightly service for women; there were speaking engagements at a girls' boarding school; quiet afternoons for guiders and a monthly service for the women whose husbands worked at the island's borstal and Parkhurst Prison. In October 1938, their ministry received further affirmation when the bishop invited them to take part in a ten-day evangelistic campaign in the Petersfield deanery.

Domestically they were reaping the rewards of their extensive garden, with Teresa reporting in the October newsletter: "The gardening Sisters have seen God's abundant blessing on all they have done, and we have all proved that peas and beans and salads which have been tended with prayerful labour respond fully to such treatment!"

Their progress towards self-sufficiency included the rearing of ducks by Sister Faith and the weaving of cloth on a Swedish handloom by Sister Bernadine, with the intention of selling any surplus to raise funds for the community. Years later Teresa recalled: "It was here that we began to live the country life that has now become the fixed pattern of our labour for our support."

The fruitfulness of the garden was reflected in the growth of the community, with the two postulants taking their vocations further by being clothed and taking the names Sister Clare and Sister Catherine. The FSJM seemed to have finally found a settled way of life when world

---

* Milton Abbey is only 17 miles away from Hinton Martell, so it is possible Dorothy Poole first met the Sisters when they were in Dorset.

events intervened. The sixth newsletter, dated St Francistide[*] 1939, found Teresa speculating:

> We do not know what exterior activities God may lead us to during the war—probably there will be some requests for a Sister to speak to groups of women, and we expect to visit a hospital at Ventnor, but transport in the Island is very difficult at present, and may limit such activities.

Teresa was right to assume that war conditions would hamper the Sisters' contact with the wider community. However, although they were cut off from the Externs on the mainland, their ministry on the island continued to develop in response to the challenges of a country at war. During the first months of the conflict, they provided a home to four young girls evacuated from Portsmouth and in March 1940 took part in a very successful ten-day parochial mission at Cowes. Recalling the event 30 years later, Teresa observed:

> The war was in full swing and many people were working overtime in the shipyards, but the mission was quite surprisingly well attended and had some good results. We visited of course, for a large part of the day, and held a service every evening in the church hall. The first Sunday evening the hall was comfortably full, and on the second it was crowded out.

There was an additional outcome of the Cowes mission, one of great future significance for the FSJM. One of the confirmation candidates at the start of the mission was a 13-year-old girl, Dorothy Inskip, who was to join the Sisters a few years later, eventually becoming Teresa's successor as head of the order.

The Isle of Wight, which had seemed so idyllic when they first arrived after the deprivations of the City Road, had in a few brief months become a place of fear and uncertainty. Teresa recalled:

---

[*] From 17 September to 4 October.

> It was an uneasy time on the Island, for the German planes came over most nights on their way to Portsmouth and Southampton and the air raid alarms seemed to be sounded several times a day. We often had to watch out in the garden for falling shrapnel and there was the bombing of convoys regularly every week for a time.

In the September 1940 newsletter, Teresa reported they had been advised by the Evacuation Authorities to have a temporary home prepared on the mainland, but they would not leave the island unless they were compulsorily evacuated. Despite the danger of their current situation, if they had stayed in London things would have been even worse. Teresa reported to her readers in October:

> We have recently heard that both of the churches which we knew best in City Road, St Clements, to which we so often went for spiritual support and peace, and St Matthew's, where we worked for five hectic years, and where Sister Margaret and I made our Life Vows, are no more, having been destroyed by bombs.

Teresa's pacifism, which led her as a young woman to join the Fellowship of Reconciliation, had not weakened over the years. When war was first announced, she wrote an article for the newsletter entitled "Pacifists or Peacemakers?", in which she stated: "A pacifist should, it seems to me, be ready to lose anything and everything rather than use the methods of the world for acquiring and keeping possession of anything, life itself included." In August 1940, she accepted an invitation to speak at the Anglican Pacifist Fellowship (APF) Conference at Whan Cross.[*] The APF, founded in 1937, was led by Dick Sheppard, the former Dean of Canterbury and prominent pacifist, and counted among its supporters such eminent figures as Evelyn Underhill, George Lansbury and Vera Brittain.[4] It is illustrative of the high regard in which Teresa was held within the pacifist community that she was invited to join the governing body of the APF. Speaking at the conference gave her the opportunity

---

[*] A retreat house near Chalfont St Giles, Buckinghamshire, run by the National Society for Promoting Christian Education.

once again to use her powerful gift for oratory which had previously so impressed the FoR during the difficult years following the First World War.

News of Teresa's pacifism reached the ears of Dom Benedict Ley OSB, who at this point was warden to the FSJM. On the instruction of the Father Abbot of his order,* he asked Teresa to give up her position on the governing body of the APF. Teresa agreed to do so, but made it clear her pacifist convictions remained. This resulted in a difficult correspondence culminating in the abbot refusing to allow his order to be associated with a community who were advising young men to resist conscription. Teresa's response was robust: "We felt we had as much moral right to advise against it if a young man's conscience was troubled, as he had to advise in favour of conscription." This prompted the abbot to withdraw Dom Benedict as their warden. However, a happy corollary of this dispute was a rapprochement between Teresa and Father Robert Andrews, now serving in a parish in Hampshire, who agreed to become their new warden.

In autumn 1940, quite unexpectedly, the Sisters were approached by the vicar with a request to train the church choir. Writing in the October newsletter, Teresa optimistically observed:

> This work brings us into close touch with some of our fellow communicants, and we hope will be the basis of a real and lasting spiritual bond of friendship between them and us; village life has its own particular problems and relationships, and we feel that in this fresh contact with the church-going folk, there is an opportunity for us of entering more fully into the life of the village, and for some such opportunity we have waited and prayed ever since we came here three years ago.

Further integration into village life followed with the Sisters holding a kindergarten each Sunday for the very young children of the church and Sister Clare, a qualified nurse, teaching first aid to the senior boys and girls at the village school. They became more involved in the local war

---

* The Benedictine Community of Nashdom Abbey.

effort, taking on the role of Air Raid Precautions (ARP) wardens: policing the blackout and using St Francis House as a first aid post. Taking the government's exhortation to "dig for victory" to heart, they took over the garden of an absent neighbour, extending their vegetable production.

Despite the constant worry of the ongoing hostilities, Teresa took great pleasure in watching the FSJM grow into the community she had envisaged: an amalgam of the parish work and religious instruction they performed in Paisley and the City Road and the productive, rural toil she had experienced at Duxford. In the November 1940 newsletter, she wrote: "Always I have felt that a village was the most natural and right setting for our type of communal life, and I hope we may be allowed to live in a village for the rest of our earthly pilgrimage!" The year ended with a well-received nativity play (no doubt influenced by the highly successful plays produced by Bernard Walke at St Hilary) and a gratifying response to an appeal for funds, which brought in £17 from the Externs.

The beginning of 1941 saw the Sisters preoccupied with the ill health of Sister Margaret, requiring treatment at the Forbes Fraser Hospital near Bath. Margaret made a good recovery, and for much of 1941 the community were able to develop further the range of their activities. They took on work in the sacristy, began confirmation classes, expanded the kindergarten and put on an Easter Tableaux with the local children. In the May newsletter, Teresa painted a picture of a contented and industrious community:

> Sister Bernadine is busy weaving at present, Sister Faith is developing a fine talent for carpentering ... Sister Margaret is so much better. Sister Clare has a pleasant little job in the village for the exercise of her nursing, Sister Catherine is becoming a good gardener, and I am full of hopes and plans and dreams and prayers.

Unfortunately, not long after writing on such a positive note, Teresa found herself once again at loggerheads with the vicar. She recalled: "Our Vicar who had seemed quite pleased with what we were doing in the parish, sacristy work, choir training, and the little Sunday school, suddenly lost his temper and was outrageously rude over the question of a Mass I had taught the choir at his request." Such was his animosity the Sisters felt they had no choice but to withdraw from all their parish work. The consequent loss of the choir went down badly in the village, with the Sisters receiving the blame. Despite the souring of local relations, that summer witnessed the ending of another clerical rift when Father Gofton Salmond came to conduct a retreat for the Sisters.

By early autumn, relations with the vicar had worsened. Teresa recalled he was "inimical to us in every way". From the start of his ministry in Whitwell, the vicar had been determined to dispense with the High Church practices of his predecessor, even preaching a sermon voicing his desire to make a bonfire of all the vestments. Teresa concluded the only reason he accepted the appointment to a parish where a daily Mass was expected was his hope the country air would benefit his delicate health. Despite his opposition, the daily Mass remained a requirement of his ministry until, due to the shortage of available teachers, he was asked to assist at the grammar school in Newport.

It was against this background of increasing tension and the loss of the daily Mass, which was such an important feature of their community's life, that Teresa found herself idly looking through the personal column of the *Daily Telegraph* on 24 October. Suddenly her eye was caught by an item advertising the sale of a "Typical thatched Devon Manor House".

Notes

[1] "St Mary's House", *Whitwell History: Isle of Wight*, <http://whitwellhistory.co.uk/history/>, accessed 22 April 2022.

[2] M. Cropper, *The Life of Evelyn Underhill* (Woodstock: Skylight Paths Publishing, 2003), p. 119.

[3] *The Times*, Friday, 25 November 1938; p. 16; Issue 48161; col E.

[4] "Anglican Pacifist Fellowship", Wikipedia (last modified 31 March 2023), <https://en.wikipedia.org/wiki/Anglican_Pacifist_Fellowship>, accessed 5 May 2023.

Part 2

CHAPTER 10

"Not imposbury but very difficult"

Considering the size of the Posbury estate, the house had 17 bedrooms and stood in over 30 acres of grounds, the price of £3,250[*] seemed very reasonable. Accordingly, with the encouragement of her fellow Sisters, Teresa wrote to request the particulars. By return of post she received a glowing description of the house and estate ending with the words: "In fact, an unspoilt piece of Devon Country." This, she shortly found out, was the only completely accurate statement in the letter. The shameless marketing, however, achieved its desired purpose and Teresa braved the vagaries and dangers of wartime travel to see for herself whether the "typical thatched Devon manor house" in the tiny hamlet of Posbury in Mid Devon could provide a suitable future home for the FSJM.

On arriving in Exeter, she discovered no one at the Globe Hotel where she was staying had ever heard of Posbury. Unfortunately, the only travel directions supplied by the agent had been the vague statement it was "somewhere between Exeter and the town of Crediton". Matters did not improve the following morning when, boarding the bus to Crediton, the conductor stated he had never heard of the place. At that point, her luck turned. One of her fellow passengers, hearing the name Posbury, told Teresa she knew the place well as she had been in service there as a young woman. She advised her to alight at Crediton station, from where she would need to walk three miles to her destination.

Setting out from the station in the late autumn sunshine, after a mile she paused on a low brick bridge to look at the water. At this moment, a car drew up and the driver offered her a lift, surprised to discover they were both headed in the same direction. Any passing thoughts Teresa

---

[*] The equivalent of £170,200 today.

may have had about the serendipity of this encounter were banished when he remarked bluntly: "You're not going to buy it are you? You won't like it."

In those days, Posbury House, which stands on a small plateau of land towards the brow of a steep hillside, could be approached from two directions. The formal entrance was to the east, marked by a lodge house from which the drive climbed steeply for half a mile through fields and the woodland of Posbury Copse. The former tradesmen's track was to the west and dropped down through agricultural land to the service entrance at the rear of the house. Teresa approached from the east:

> We turned in at the Lodge gates and I wondered how grand the place was for we went up the drive which looked wonderful in all the beauty of Autumn colour and it seemed a long way. I imagined wrought iron gates and a great oak door and nearly laughed aloud when we stopped at the bottom of the steps and walked up between the tall rhododendrons and in at the very unpretentious front door into the hall with its stone floor, looking much more like a farm-house than a mansion.

In fact, Posbury House was neither mansion, manor house nor farmhouse but a *cottage ornée*. Buildings of this type were constructed between the late-eighteenth and mid-nineteenth centuries as retreats for wealthy families whose opportunities for travel had been restricted, first by the French Revolution and then by the Napoleonic Wars.[1] They were almost always built in places of natural beauty and included a mix of vernacular and whimsical features such as decorative thatched roofs, small-paned casement windows and gothick-style wrought ironwork. Posbury House was characteristic of the type: an early-nineteenth-century two-storey building with a pretty hipped thatched roof projecting into a conical extension over a double height bay on its southeast garden façade. It had tall casement windows, some with leaded diamond panes, and a veranda with decorative wrought iron supports giving onto the garden, woodland and wider setting of farmland. Its immediate setting of a charming ornamental garden with a small lake was the epitome of the Picturesque.

The land on which the *cottage ornée* was built originally formed part of the de Posbury family manor. However, by the time of the building's construction the land was part of the Shobrooke Park estate owned by Sir Richard Hippisley Tuckfield. As part of the development of the small Posbury estate, in 1835 Sir Richard made the philanthropic gesture of building a chapel of ease for the church of Holy Cross, Crediton. St Luke's Chapel, built of local volcanic stone in the style of the Gothic Revival, was sited directly above the field to the north of the new *cottage ornée*. A year later, Sir Richard's wife, Lady Charlotte, founded a school close to the chapel for the training of teachers, known as St Luke's College.[*]

The chapel's curate, who was also headteacher at the school, lived with his students at Priestcott, a five-bedroom house lying in a field to the south-east of the chapel, approached from the rear drive to Posbury House. The style of the house with its local stone walls, thatch and Picturesque features, in this case a Tudor-style panelled front door and elegant arched stair window, was similar to Posbury Lodge, suggesting they were all part of the original design for the small estate. Posbury House and grounds, along with 1,800 acres of surrounding farmland, farms and cottages, were put up for sale at auction on behalf of the Hippisley Tuckfields on 3 May 1940. Posbury Lodge and Priestcott were sold as separate lots,[†] but at the end of the sale the "Attractive Old-World Residence" of Posbury House remained unsold.

Teresa was probably unaware of the small estate's former connection with the Anglican Church before her first visit, although undoubtedly the close proximity of the small chapel must have been a happy discovery. Less encouraging, however, was the condition of the main building. She later recalled: "The whole place had a 'knocked about' air, partly because in a house which can hold twenty people with reasonable comfort, there were forty boys and ten adults." The occupants were the staff and pupils of the Beacon School, Teignmouth, who had been evacuated to the house following an air raid in 1940. The boys were still in residence when Teresa was shown around and she later recalled "there was a bed, or a boy,

---

[*] The small training college was relocated to the Cathedral Close, Exeter in 1839 and the building was subsequently used as a Sunday school.

[†] Posbury Lodge sold for £130 and Priestcott sold for £550.

or a desk in every corner". Her guide was the headmaster's wife, Mrs Daunt, who kept up a discouraging commentary throughout her tour. Teresa, however, saw past the superficial wear and tear, picturing the great potential of the place. She was particularly taken with the former stable block, now converted into a games room, which she felt would be eminently suitable as a chapel.

During lunch with the boys, Mr and Mrs Daunt continued to point out the shortcomings of the place. But by now deep in the throes of the infatuation prospective buyers feel when they have found "the one", Teresa only attended to their one positive statement, "that there was always some flower or shrub blossoming in the garden all the year round". Viewing the garden after lunch, whilst noting its sadly overgrown and neglected state, she was enchanted by the autumnal colours of the mature larches, beeches and oaks. By the end of the afternoon, while under no illusion of the scale of the project, she felt nevertheless "a quiet sense that this was probably our place". The idyllic setting, thatched buildings and extensive grounds, with its echoes of Duxhurst, a place where she had seen the troubled find refuge and spiritual healing, may have fostered this sense of certainty.

Returning to Exeter, she sent a telegram to her Sisters: "Not imposbury but very difficult"—a play on the words uttered by Father Lucius Clay 17 years previously when she shared with him her hopes of founding an order.

On her return to the island, Teresa continued to ponder the feasibility of the FSJM moving to Devon, including: the scale of renovation required by a relatively small number of women; the property's remoteness; no daily Mass unless they could employ their own chaplain; and the not inconsiderable difficulty of the community's lack of funds. Despite these concerns, she remained certain that Posbury should be their new home but wanted Sister Margaret, as the only other Sister at that time in life vows, to view the property before any further steps were taken.

There could not have been a greater contrast between Teresa's first viewing of Posbury and that of Sister Margaret. They arrived on 6 December in pouring rain, which did not cease for the duration of their visit. The school staff, busy with their preparations to move out, were harassed and the house was in a terrible state. As the Sisters trailed from room to room amongst the packing cases and piles of rubbish, Sister Margaret grew increasingly silent. There was nowhere inside for them to sit, so they ended up perched on a garden seat under the dripping veranda looking across the rain-sodden lawn. After sitting in silence for some time and feeling increasingly cold, Sister Margaret suddenly burst into tears, declaring: "Mother, I don't know how you can think we can possibly take over a place like this."

Sister Margaret's negative reaction must have been a blow for Teresa, but she respected her friend's opinion and agreed they should waste no more time on the enterprise and call for a taxi. As they set off down the dark, dank drive, which only a month earlier had so enchanted Teresa with its autumnal beauty, Margaret began to question her response. She fretted it might be God's will that they should come to Devon, so perhaps her reservations should be discounted. As the taxi journeyed towards Exeter, through the beautiful valley of the River Creedy and the picturesque village of Newton St Cyres, her mood began to lift. By the time they reached Exeter, she had experienced a complete volte face, declaring: "Mother, do forgive me for being so silly, of course you must try and get that place."

Accordingly, the next day Teresa and Sister Margaret called on the Rector of Crediton, the Revd Francis Richards, to find out how frequently services were held at St Luke's Chapel and whether Mass might be said at Posbury if they were to set up their own chapel. The rector, polite but not enthusiastic, said he would be prepared to welcome them and make sure they had one Mass a week at their chapel, as long as they had the "approval and sanction" of the Bishop of Exeter. By great good fortune, the former Bishop of Stepney, Charles Curzon, who had supported the Sisters during their time at City Road, had been appointed Bishop of Exeter in 1936, making them confident of episcopal approval.

Following their return to the Isle of Wight, Sister Margaret took the initiative in hastening the move. She wrote to Max Batten, the Sisters' solicitor in London, who duly commissioned a thorough condition survey of Posbury House. The resulting report stated rather discouragingly that the house had "no architectural features within or without", and less surprisingly that its current poor condition meant it was not worth the asking price. Mr Batten advised against taking the purchase any further, but after Sister Margaret replied, "God meant us to go to Posbury if possible", he moved into business mode and began to haggle on their behalf.

As so often before in times of stress, Teresa became ill and was in bed for nearly a fortnight with severe headaches. Finally, their reduced offer of £2,250* was accepted but, rather than feelings of relief, Teresa was assailed by doubts. In her account of the purchase, Teresa records it was only at this point they began to consider from where the necessary funds to purchase Posbury could be found. However, it seems probable she was already fully aware that Sister Margret could be approached for financial assistance if necessary. In the event, Sister Margaret contacted her brother, as she had done previously when they wished to purchase the lease of the Oakley Crescent house in London. He agreed to loan her the remaining money from the future sale of their mother's house, which amounted to £1,800. The remaining £500 came in the form of an interest-free loan from a wealthy priest friend who was living on the island. The contract for the house was signed on 11 February 1942, a date Teresa considered of great significance, as it was the Feast of Our Lady's Apparition at Lourdes.

Although the lease of their Whitwell house did not end until September, Teresa was anxious the community should move to Posbury as soon as possible in order to prepare the land for sowing vegetables in the spring. The decision to leave early was made easier by the fortuitous requisitioning of the Whitwell house by the army.

As she was still not feeling physically robust, Teresa left her fellow Sisters to close up the house on the island, travelling to Exeter in late February, where she stayed with the Sisters of the Community of St Wilfrid. From here she journeyed back and forth by bus to Crediton, establishing contacts with the local tradespeople and taking stock of what needed to be done. Following the departure of the school, the lamentable state of the building was evident: "It was a rather dismaying sight, the whole house looked dirty and with all the furniture gone I could see the knocked-about walls and other horrors." At this point, Teresa was joined by the two young Sisters, Clare and Catherine, who had both

---

* The equivalent of £117,830 today.

taken their first vows the previous November. She recalled them arriving at the station in Exeter, alighting from the train dressed in their habits with their hands full of buckets and brooms, much to the astonishment of the passengers waiting on the platform.

The three Sisters moved into the Ship Hotel in Crediton and for an exhausting week walked the three miles to Posbury, where they spent the whole day sorting and cleaning, before facing the long walk back to their digs. As the week progressed, word of the Sisters' travails spread through the local community and resulted in the offer of the use of Priestcott (the former home of the curate of St Luke's which lay just over the field from Posbury House). This allowed the Sisters to spend all their time and energy making the house habitable, as a consequence of which they were able to spend the night in their new home when the first load of furniture was delivered on 5 March. The second shipment arrived two days later along with Sisters Margaret, Bernadine, Faith and a young woman named Violet who had been staying with them on the island.

There was an immense amount of work to do in the house and grounds, but the Sisters' first priority was to convert the former stable, recently used as a playroom, into a chapel. Teresa was determined the original character of the building should be retained, observing: "This will help us to keep in mind the simplicity and lowliness of Our Lord's first earthly home, and so guard us from ever desiring a fine Chapel with furnishings not in accordance with our vocation."

The Church Union, an Anglo-Catholic advocacy group, provided altar linen, two sets of vestments, a crucifix and albs, and one of the Externs gave them money to purchase candlesticks. On 5 April, in Easter Week, enough order had been established for a blessing ceremony of the house and chapel, which was dedicated to The Most Precious Blood, to take place conducted by the Rector of Crediton. The Sisters had received approval from the Bishop of Exeter for the Reserved Sacrament to be held in the chapel—this permission was a significant development for Teresa in the building of the community she had envisaged:

> We feel that our happiness is complete in our new home, for we have Him whom our souls desire to love, dwelling here with us in such a homely, intimate way, and it is such a joyful satisfaction

to be able to offer Him all of the loveliness of these thirty-one acres of land.

A fortnight later, on 22 April, the chapel was the scene of another important event, when the Bishop of Crediton, William Surtees, received the life vows of Sister Bernadine and consecrated the altar. Joining the Sisters in the ceremony were two significant figures in the formation of the FSJM: their warden, Father Robert, and former warden, Father Salmond. With a fully operational chapel and three Sisters now in life vows, life for the FSJM at Posbury had got off to a promising start.

Notes

[1] Daniel Maudlin, *The Idea of the Cottage in English Architecture, 1760–1860* (Abingdon: Routledge, 2015), p. 161.

CHAPTER 11

Posbury St Francis: Prayer and work

At last, the FSJM had found a permanent home—but what form would community life take? Teresa, who was now known as Mother, offered the following profound but non-specific mission statement: "Posbury was given to me by God, to be used and cared for as a tiny part of His Kingdom on earth, and to be shared as far as possible with all whom came our way." She had always remained unwavering in her quest to build a new type of community, based on the calling which 20 years before she had received at St Hilary.

This desire, however, was to be put to the test shortly after the FSJM arrived in Devon when they were approached by the Society of St Francis (SSF), in the person of Father Algy Robertson, a senior friar within the order. The SSF had been formed in the 1930s with the purpose of drawing together a number of the existing Anglican Franciscan groups into one Franciscan Society. Father Algy was the warden of the Community of Francis, the women's branch of the SSF, and was eager for the FSJM to become affiliated to the order.

The approach from the SSF was undoubtedly an indication the FSJM were now considered a legitimate order, and the offer to be taken under the wing of an established organization must have had its attractions. However, the Sisters were unanimous in their desire to retain their independence. Father Algy then advised them to consider setting up a trust to act as administrators for the order, which would free them from the responsibilities of ownership. Once again, they demurred. Teresa later explained their decision had been influenced by their meeting with the Italian Larks of St Francis, who had taken sole responsibility for the ownership of their property and the running of their community; a decision which had enabled them to pursue a ministry free from any outside considerations or constraints. So the FSJM decided to remain fully independent: a decision which greatly influenced its resultant idiosyncratic character.

One of the most obvious signs of the "otherness" of the community was their brown habits, by this point hand-woven by Sister Bernadine; more akin to the robes of Franciscan monks than the dark habits typically worn by Anglican nuns. At some point after they moved to Devon, the starched white cornettes were replaced with winged brown headdresses, fashioned from a stiff material, which sat above the wimple. These elaborate headdresses, somewhere on the cusp between forbidding and comical, were certainly distinctive and gave the FSJM an instant unique identity.

The naming of their new home was equally unconventional. Teresa was determined they should not use the term "convent", so the house was renamed Posbury St Francis. Equally forbidden was the term "nun". Other than Teresa, who was "Mother", all the other women associated with the order were referred to as "Sister", with Teresa frequently making no differentiation in terminology between those who lived in community and the Externs. Confusingly, Sister Faith, who lived as part of the community, was an Extern, her different status defined only by her dress. She wore the Extern habit of ordinary clothes, covered by a skirt-length scapular belted with a white cord with a single knot symbolizing obedience.

Similarly, the pattern of life did not follow the example of existing Anglican orders, but took its inspiration directly from the life of St Francis. Teresa stated:

> We endeavour to live a balanced life of prayer and work, giving the chief place to prayer, for no spiritual work can be of any use or value unless it springs from faith, hope and charity, which can only be planted in our souls and minds through union with God in prayer.

Her resolve to ground the community life in prayer saw the FSJM adopt a daily schedule similar to the Roman Catholic tradition of the Divine Office. Each morning the Sisters would take it in turns to ring a waking bell at 6.30 a.m., following which they would assemble in the chapel for Lauds at 7 a.m. If there was a priest in residence, this would be followed at

8 a.m. by Mass. The next two offices of the day, Prime and Terce, would be said privately before noon, when the Sisters who worked outside would recite Sext—either in the chapel or where they were working, having been summoned by a cowbell. The Sisters who worked inside the house said None after their lunchtime meal (referred to as dinner). They would all assemble in the chapel after supper to say Vespers before retuning just before bed for Compline. Throughout the day, periods of prayer would be allotted to each Sister, resulting in an almost constant offering of prayer within the chapel during the day.

Coterminous with the life of prayer was the life of work. Initially there was the daunting task of sorting out and then maintaining the house and grounds. Teresa firmly believed the labours of housework and gardening were fundamental to the Franciscan life, referring to it as the "original spiritual work", and was disdainful of anyone who queried the appropriateness of religious spending their days planting trees and digging. In a newsletter, Teresa noted the manual work at Posbury was allocated according to the Sisters' aptitude and physical capabilities. To begin with, Sisters Margaret, Catherine and Faith worked in the garden, while the others carried out the laundry, cooking and cleaning. It is possible that another factor influenced the division of labour. There persisted, despite so many former domestic servants being redeployed for the war effort, the lingering convention that gardening was a suitable pastime for a lady, but housework most certainly was not. All the Sisters, however, were faced with an enormous challenge: the house required extensive repairs and redecorating, and although part of the vegetable garden had been kept in good order by the school, the rest of the grounds were very overgrown.

They planned to take on no additional work until the house and grounds were restored, but on 4 May 1942 international events intervened. Exeter suffered a terrible and sustained air raid, which led to 156 deaths, 563 injured and 30 acres of the city destroyed.[1] Among the many buildings lost was St Luke's College (the successor to the original teacher training college sited in the Posbury valley).[*] St Luke's was the

---

[*] Also destroyed was the Globe Hotel where Teresa had stayed on her first visit to Exeter.

venue for the annual ordination candidates' retreat for the Diocese of Exeter, which was due to be held that year at the end of June. With this date fast approaching, Bishop Curzon contacted Teresa to enquire whether Posbury might host the retreat. Mother, although concerned about the lack of furniture and the suitability of the tiny chapel, rose to the challenge and just three months after their arrival in Devon the FSJM hosted the bishop, two priests and seven ordinands.

As a direct consequence, the community at Posbury was not only assimilated overnight into the established life of the Diocese of Exeter, but also thrust onto the radar of several national institutions. That same year in September they received a request from the National Society (the Church of England Education Office) to host a training course for priests and deacons. The National Society courses became a regular fixture, attended by up to 14 delegates, and proved an important source of income. By October, 70 people had stayed in the house, sleeping in cells vacated by the Sisters, who camped out in other rooms. At the time, the Sisters' decision to live alongside their retreatants was considered revolutionary and borderline scandalous. Teresa later reflected:

> The idea of a man in the house was something quite terrible then, and we were the bad girls for years and years because right from the beginning we had men in the house. Of course partly my view of men, having done the kind of work I had, was quite different from the ordinary Sisters' view of men.

The hosting of retreats, conferences and Quiet Days became a significant part of the "work" carried out by the FSJM. Each year from mid-Lent until St Francistide the Sisters accommodated retreats for priests, women's groups, parishes and organizations such as the Mothers' Union, the Anglican Pacifists and Toc H.* From the end of October the community was closed to visitors, apart from the weeks from 1–13 January when they were joined by friends and some of the Externs. During this period, they

---

* An interdenominational Christian movement which sought to ease the burdens of others through acts of service and to promote cohesion throughout society.

began the practice of "the Epiphany draw", where each person living in the house would draw from the crib in the chapel a card with the name of a saint who would become their patron for that year.

Although Teresa stated there was no written Rule at this point, there were a number of principles to which the community adhered. These were: no fixed charges for accommodation—guests were asked to pay according to their means; the holding of no invested funds; no recourse to law if anything was taken from them; and no engagement with any war efforts.

This last principle reflected Teresa's long-standing commitment to pacifism and was non-negotiable. All Sisters looking to join the FSJM had to be committed pacifists—a requirement which distinguished them from other religious orders. Further indicators of their commitment to the pacifist cause included their hosting of the Anglican Pacifist Conference and Retreat at the end of April 1943. Later in the war, they took in an Italian prisoner of war, known as Porta, from a nearby camp to help in their newly created market garden. Teresa was not particularly impressed by his work ethic but amused by his referring to her as "grandmother"—a not inappropriate description as the attractive and spirited young woman had become a redoubtable and sturdy middle-aged matron with an imposing air of authority.

In September 1945, Porta was replaced by a German prisoner of war, Wilhelm, who swiftly impressed Mother with his industry. In no time, he was absorbed into community life and for Christmas 1945 presented the Sisters with a candlestand he had fashioned based on the triangular design of the Roman Catholic Tenebræ Hearse. Such was the closeness of the relationship between Wilhelm and the community that, when he voiced concerns that his fellow Catholic prisoners of war had not received the Sacrament for months, Mother contacted the Abbot of Buckfast. He promptly sent a German-speaking priest to the camp to hear their confessions and take them communion.

Mother saw the gift of the candlestand, which could hold 15 votive candles, as an opportunity to promote the FSJM's principles of reconciliation on a national scale. She wrote an article, published in the *Church Times*, in which she described the gift from Wilhelm and encouraged the readers to send requests for prayers in the cause of peace, penitence and unity. She then sent a copy of the article, translated by Wilhelm into German, to George Bell, the Bishop of Chichester, who at this time was involved in helping interned Germans and British conscientious objectors. He in turn gave the article to a German pastor he knew who was returning to Germany so it could be disseminated among members of the German resistance.

Soon after their arrival in Devon, another cause close to Teresa's heart required support from the FSJM. In October 1942, the governor of HMP Exeter enquired whether they would be able to assist with prison visiting and the conducting of services in the prison chapel. HMP Exeter at this time was temporarily housing women inmates, due to an increase in criminal convictions, and the prison chaplain was struggling. The women prisoners had not responded well to him, and the governor hoped the Sisters might be able to make a better connection. The work was quite arduous, entailing three hours visiting the women in their cells on Saturday afternoons and a service followed by more visits on Sunday. Teresa and Sister Margaret took it in turns to provide the service and were eventually joined in the rota by Sister Bernadine in 1944.

Many of the women were very young and had been convicted for sexual offences. Teresa noted:

> Very few of them have any deliberate intention of going wrong... hardly any one of them seems to have any grip on reality, either spiritual or material. A prison sentence does not help them find reality, in spite of a conventional theory that a dose of prison brings people up against hard facts! The one thing prison can do in the way of construction is to give those it receives time to think, but even this gift has usually to be stirred up by someone who comes from outside!

She worried that they did not seem to get through to many of the women, but continued with the work as an act of love, penitence and reparation. In fact, attendance at the Sunday services was quite high and at Whitsun 1943 three of the inmates were confirmed. The Sisters' prison ministry was not confined to their work on the estate: for a few months they cared for the eight-year-old daughter of an inmate and provided a home for a newly released prisoner until she was able to find work and a place of her own.

In addition to their prison work, the FSJM sought to reach out to the wider community in Devon through hospital visiting and speaking at Mothers' Union meetings. They were given permission from the Bishop of Exeter to give addresses in churches with the agreement of the local incumbent and Sister Margaret began a regular ministry once a month in a poor parish in Devonport. They revived their mission work with a mission to Meeth in West Devon, where there was a strong tradition of Nonconformity and a trenchant atmosphere of mutual suspicion between the chapel- and church-going communities. This opportunity to put her theories on ecumenism into practice would have greatly appealed to Teresa, and the Anglican incumbent, Father Fry, considered the resultant rapprochement between the two denominations a great success. If a speech or talk were required it was usually given by Teresa or Sister Margaret, but as their commitments grew, they were joined by Sister Bernadine.

In 1943, Sister Margaret's mother died and she received an inheritance. As the FSJM rules forbad the holding of investments, the funds were used for a number of capital projects which the Sisters felt would enhance the development of the community. The chapel, so swiftly first brought into commission, was extended to encompass the adjoining former boiler room which was converted into a sacristy. The rudimentary stools the Sisters had sat on during services were replaced with stalls constructed by the local builder, Mr Francis,* who also built the altar, for the reasonable fee of £38.

Their next expenditure was the purchase of Posbury Clump—a small area of woodland which had previously been sold in the auction of the

---

* The firm Dart & Francis was very well known both locally and nationally, with distinctive late-nineteenth-century Tudor/Gothic premises on Crediton High Street. They were contractors for a number of churches designed by significant nineteenth-century architects in Devon, the most notable of which was St Davids in Exeter by Caröe. Until the late 1980s, they produced ecclesiastical fittings on a national scale, and still operate from their original premises.

Posbury estate in May 1940. On hearing the present owner intended to cut down the trees, the Sisters determined to save the local nature area and put in a successful offer. This was quite a significant purchase: the 1940 sales catalogue described Posbury Clump, Lot 45, as "a useful mixed wood comprising over four acres with 104 oaks, 228 Scots pine, 57 ash and 21 larch", and it sold for £200. Perched on the top of the hillside across the valley from the community, Posbury Clump was a significant landmark and an area of great natural beauty, later to be designated a site of special scientific interest.

The decision to purchase Posbury Clump when so many other more practical works required funding was illustrative of the Sisters' alternative priorities: the desire to follow literally the example of St Francis, who had spent his life worshipping God in nature as much as in church. Teresa felt Posbury Clump, with its ancient trees and forest floor studded with wildflowers, had a special atmosphere which would be conducive to prayer and contemplation.

The final purchase with Sister Margaret's inheritance was of a more practical nature—a small, detached house situated opposite St Luke's Chapel. Known as Woodlands, it was renamed Lord's Meadow and used as additional accommodation for the Sisters when Posbury House was full of retreatants. An additional boost to their coffers came from Sister Margaret's brother, Dr George Buckley, who on receiving his own inheritance gifted them £1,000 to buy much-needed mechanical equipment including a small tractor, circular saw and an auto-scythe.

Posbury provided the perfect environment for the Sisters' commitment to living a Franciscan life. To Sister Faith's ducks brought from the Isle of Wight they added chickens, bees and, towards the end of the war, pigs. They had a dog called Bonnie, named after the local saint Boniface, and two cats, Dominic and Katie, whose antics were frequently recorded in the newsletter, often incongruously juxtaposed with weighty religious comment. The vegetable plot was extended into a full-size market garden in a former field known as Greenclose. Here they grew a variety of fruit and vegetables for themselves and the retreatants, with the surplus sold through a shop in Crediton. Despite the necessity of concentrating on food production due to the wartime restrictions, the Sisters also managed to restore the long border, one of the major elements of the original *cottage ornée* garden, which they christened St Anthony's Border.

The transformation of the garden and grounds at Posbury was greatly facilitated by the arrival of a young woman called Mary Cope. She first came to Posbury to attend the Anglican Pacifist Conference in April 1943, but had subsequently kept in touch, eventually deciding to join the Sisters in October 1944. She was interested in a life of prayer and manual work, but initially did not wish to test whether she had a vocation to the Sisterhood. Mary, a trained horticulturalist and graduate of the well-regarded Studley Horticultural and Agricultural College for Women, had formerly been working as a gardener at a girls' school. The combination of her youth—she was 27 years old—and knowledge had a transformative effect on the Sisters' outdoor endeavours. As she worked away planning and constructing the market garden and overseeing the clearing of years of undergrowth to reveal the elegant lines of the formal garden, her commitment to the FSJM intensified. In November 1944, she took the decision to become an Extern novice and a year later a postulant.

In addition to her horticultural prowess, she brought another great benefit to the community in the form of a driving license. Previously the Sisters had been reliant on lifts or taxis into Crediton to get provisions or to go to church on the three Sundays a month when there was no service at St Luke's. If no lift was available, they would walk, coming home via the evocatively named Breakheart Hill, described by Mother as "a pretty but very tiring proposition".

Another significant new addition to the community during the early years at Posbury was Dorothy Inskip, the young girl the Sisters first met at her confirmation in Cowes in 1940. Like Mary, Dorothy had kept in contact and in April 1942, aged just 15, was accepted as a probationer Extern. As her background was somewhat unsettled—she had been born illegitimate and brought up in a less than satisfactory adoptive home—Dorothy made the decision on reaching the age of 17 to make her permanent home at Posbury. She was accepted as the FSJM's youngest novice and took the name Sister Hilary of the Child Jesus, in memory of the place that held such significance in the formation of the FSJM.[*]

---

[*] All the Sisters' names were chosen by Teresa.

Teresa later recalled the early years at Posbury as a time when the Sisters were able to contribute to community life using their own particular skills: Sister Bernadine, as a trained draughtswoman, created beautiful lettering for the community's cards and documents in addition to weaving the cloth for their winter habits; Sister Clare used her artistic skills to paint pictures; Sister Margaret played the piano and the accordion for the Sisters at recreation; Sister Hilary made toys and cards; and Sister Faith wove baskets and trays, which were sold along with Sister Bernadine's cloth.

Just as it seemed that the community was set for expansion, one of the young women, Sister Catherine, decided to leave. She had joined the FSJM as a postulant in 1938, taken part in the successful 1941 Cowes mission the same year she took her first vows and, as one of the younger Sisters, had proved invaluable in the hard work sorting out the house and grounds at Posbury. Teresa made no mention of the reason for her departure in the newsletters but did refer to the loss of her assistance in the garden. It may have been the unrelenting hard manual work proved too much for someone with Sister Catherine's artistic talents, but the reason for her departure in summer 1944 is unknown.

Shortly after she left, the Sisters were joined by Mother Ivy and Sister Rosanna. Unfortunately, both women were now in the advanced stages of dementia, and within just a few months it was clear the community could not cope with their increasing needs. Later describing this difficult period, Teresa defended her decision to offer them a home, maintaining:

> The Community owes much more than I can ever tell to these two holy people and one could say that the thought and prayer, especially of Mother Ivy, lies at the foundation of our Life of Prayer and thought. Through them we have received a vision of the inner and real life which I pray we may never lose.

In 1945, ill health in the community was not confined to its most elderly members. Sister Clare began to suffer from periods of ill health and exhaustion. At first, the Sisters put this down to the increased workload in the garden following the departure of Sister Catherine, but eventually she was sent to the local doctor. He, however, could find nothing the matter with her and she returned to Posbury, but her health continued to decline. Eventually Sister Clare went home to her parents, where she was diagnosed with Addison's disease and within three months was dead. Teresa recalled: "It was a great blow to us and to her for she had a good and happy vocation until her illness began."

The Sisters were aware that the natural reticence of their Devonian neighbours and the constraints of wartime were hampering their assimilation into the local community. Sister Bernadine had the most success at integration, teaching spinning to the women in the neighbouring hamlet and handicrafts to the local children. However, Mother Teresa sensed the local people were not entirely reconciled to their presence and was concerned that, when the time came for their first burial, there might be resistance if they requested a plot within the restricted space of St Luke's churchyard. Accordingly, she sought permission from the Ministry of Health to create a private burial ground, having identified a suitable plot which sloped gently down to the drive to the north-east of the main lawn. Permission was granted in September 1944 and Bishop Curzon advised Mother to have the ground blessed rather than consecrated, to avoid the graveyard falling under the jurisdiction of the diocese. Always happy to remain as autonomous as possible, she followed his recommendation and, as a consequence, the land was blessed before any internment took place.

The focal point of the new burial ground was a wooden crucifix with a triangular canopy set on a plinth of stones rescued from the church of St Laurence in Exeter which was bombed during the Blitz. Due to wartime restriction, railings were out of the question, so the Sisters decided to enclose the plot with a flowering hedge of camellias, roses and rhododendrons. Fittingly, the first burial was Teresa's mentor Mother Ivy, who died in April 1945.

In the newsletter, Teresa frequently shared with their friends and Externs reminders that, whatever atrocities were occurring in the world, beauty could still be found in their secluded fold of Devon countryside. In May 1944 she wrote:

> As we work in the garden, and walk in our quiet lanes, where foxgloves are glowing and wreaths of honeysuckle filling the

air with sweetness, it is strange to think of the horror and devastation and death which is so near on the physical plane, and so immeasurably far from the spirit of this beautiful country-side.

When the cold winter of 1945 brought snow, she observed: "The whole place looked incredibly lovely, and the snow added to the sense of stillness and alone-ness which is part of the atmosphere here at all times."

To enhance this sense of a place apart, the Sisters sought to create "retired spots" throughout the grounds and surrounding woodland to encourage prayer and meditation. This project was assisted by the planting of 500 Scots pine and Douglas fir saplings, obtained from the society Men of the Trees—an organization which promoted the healing properties of nature. Some may have questioned the direction of their efforts when so many were engaged in war work, but Mother Teresa saw the venture as necessary as knitting airmen's socks or policing the blackout.

Her attitude towards the environment was remarkably prescient; in September 1945 she wrote:

> No one who is drawn to the spirit of St Francis can be other than a lover of nature, but it becomes clear to one after a time that it is not enough to love birds and beasts and flowers, one must begin to realize that they too, are part of the "worshipping community" and have their share in the vocation to praise and obey the Creator of all that is. We come to understand with sorrow and penitence that the human race is continually violating and wronging the earth, defacing its beauty and robbing it of its fruitfulness in times both of war and peace, and so something of a spirit of reparation has to enter into our labours, and our delights, in the world of nature.

Due to the strength of Teresa's vision and the sheer hard work of the Sisters, as the war drew to a close, Posbury St Francis was already established as an important centre for retreat and its distinctive character as a place apart of almost unearthly beauty had begun to emerge.

Notes

[1] "The Exeter Blitz—April and May 1942", *Exeter Memories*, <http://www.exetermemories.co.uk/em/exeterblitz.php>, accessed 1 April 2023.

CHAPTER 12

Post-war growth

A small photograph taken on 26 April 1946 shows Teresa sitting on a rustic bench which has been dragged onto the front lawn at Posbury from its usual position under the veranda. She is flanked by two young women, wearing the habit of the FSJM. The occasion is the clothing of Mary Cope (seated on Mother's right), who, after 18 months living and working at Posbury, had taken the decision to deepen her commitment to the order—taking the name in religion of Sister Mary of Our Lady of Sorrows. Seated on Mother's left is Mary Benson, who had also been clothed that day. This second Mary was the girl whose dying mother had been nursed 20 years earlier in Paisley by Teresa and Sister Margaret. In the intervening years, she had taken work in the local cotton mill to support her impoverished cobbler father, but her encounter with the Sisters clearly had a profound effect, and she maintained contact with them through her parish priest, Father Robert Andrews.

In 1945, the Sisters invited Mary Benson to spend her summer holiday with them at Posbury and during her stay she experienced a calling to enter the community. As a consequence, she joined Sister Mary in the clothing ceremony in Easter 1946 and took the name Sister Mary Bride of the Sacred Heart. Unlike Sister Mary, Sister Bride did not have any specialist skills and had little learning, but her qualities of stoic commitment and loyalty, combined with an attitude that no task was too menial or too onerous, were of tremendous value to the FSJM.

Sisters Bride and Mary, aged 34 and 29 respectively, were young and fit and their decision to commit to the order must have been a huge relief after the loss of Sisters Clare and Catherine. In the group photograph taken on the day of their clothing, they appear to be of similar height and slight build—the habit and headdress further exaggerating their similarities. More relaxed photographs taken on the same day show Sister Mary as the more animated, with a broad smile revealing prominent teeth in a deeply tanned face, testament to her days spent largely outside. Sister Bride, by contrast, appears more reserved, with large, expressive eyes and a generous mouth. The Sisters were further distinguished by their accents: Sister Mary spoke in the received pronunciation of the middle class, whereas Sister Bride had a broad Clydeside accent which she was to retain for the rest of her life.

Two further Sisters appear in the group photograph: Sister Bernadine, shortly to celebrate her 46th birthday, sitting gamely cross-legged on the ground in front of Sister Mary and, kneeling awkwardly in front of Sister Bride, a tall young woman. This is Sister Hilary, about to turn 20, already clothed for almost three years and shortly to be professed that autumn in temporary vows, the first novice to do so at Posbury. Although looking directly at the camera, Sister Hilary's slightly hunched demeanour betrays her shyness and unease at having her photograph taken. Missing from the group is Sister Margaret, who had been diagnosed with vascular disease and was thereafter to suffer periodic episodes of ill health.

The year 1946 was to prove a fruitful one for the order; they were joined in July by the postulant Elizabeth Lockhead Shaw, who took the name Sister Elizabeth of the Holy Family. Sister Elizabeth had first encountered Mother Teresa and Sister Margaret during their Paisley days at Father Robert Andrews' church services. Despite attending the same church, her background was far more comfortable than that of Sister Bride. Sister Elizabeth's father was secretary at the Coats family's Anchor Mills thread factory, and the family lived in a spacious house filled with music. Her father was a fine organist and singer, and the young Betty grew up knowing all the hymns in the *English Hymnal* by heart. In addition to music, her other love was children, which led to her work at the Smiley Day Nursery in Paisley, where she was photographed with Queen Elizabeth during a royal visit in 1941. When the Sisters left Paisley, she maintained contact, and, in 1935, became one of the early intake of Externs when the FSJM were at City Road. For the next ten years, she stayed with them on retreat before eventually, in 1946, taking the decision to leave her job and test her vocation.

With her short, sturdy build and round, smiling face Sister Elizabeth could have been mistaken for a native Devonian, until she spoke in her distinctive soft Scottish accent. Her demeanour was one of constant cheerfulness and, like her fellow Scot Sister Bride, she was more than happy to take on any menial task, be it mending and sewing inside the house or weeding and digging in the garden. She was a prodigious knitter, producing numerous complicated Aran sweaters seemingly effortlessly. Her real gift, however, was with children, and she was always at the forefront of any mission or local community work in which they were involved.

All four Sisters were to make a permanent commitment to the FSJM, with Sister Hilary making her life vows in 1949, followed by Sister Mary and Sister Bride in 1951 and Sister Elizabeth in 1954. During these years, several other women came to the community to test their vocations but did not stay. In most instances, this was because Mother did not think they had a vocation to community life, and the majority became Externs. Throughout this period, Extern Sister Violet, who had travelled to Posbury with the Sisters from the Isle of Wight, continued to live with them. She was a semi-invalid suffering with tuberculosis, but by 1955, having made a sufficient recovery to allow her to return to work, she left the community.

In 1946, Father Robert Andrews stood down as warden. He continued as the Sisters' confessor extraordinary, visiting Posbury on occasion for the next three years before returning to Scotland, where he eventually died in 1964. Despite their difficult initial relationship in the early years at Paisley, Teresa ultimately credited Father Robert as the inspiration for some of the guiding principles that underpinned the community:

> To him we owe a great debt of gratitude for his teaching on prayer, and his insistence on it as the one thing that mattered supremely. And in the first years of the existence of FSJM his breadth of spirit and outlook helped Sister Margaret and myself to keep free of the kind of piety that everyone then associated with the Life of a Sister, a piety in-looking rather than out-going. Father Robert's view about us was that anything that was right for ordinary Christians was right for us. Also from him we learned to see that

contemplative prayer can be practised without the support and withdrawal of enclosure, though as he said one day to me "It is a crucifying Life, but it can be lived". These words of Father Robert set a seal on my own thoughts and strivings and pointed to the vocation of the Franciscan Servants of Jesus and Mary.

Father Robert was succeeded as warden by Father John Hooper, the Rector of Kenn, a small parish to the south of Exeter. Father Hooper was well known in the diocese for his extensive library and thought-provoking sermons. A committed Anglo-Catholic, he lived a celibate, ascetic life and was sought out by his fellow priests for his theological learning and spiritual guidance. When the fiercely intellectual Bishop Robert Mortimer succeeded Bishop Curzon in 1949 as Bishop of Exeter, he chose to attend Kenn Church on his rare free Sundays to hear Father Hooper preach. Slight of build, with a quizzical expression, Hooper appears in the back row of the group photograph taken after the clothing of Sisters Mary and Bride; the first ceremony at which he officiated as warden. He was a perceptive man and under no illusions about the challenges the Sisters faced. Teresa recalled: "Father John once said to me that he thought much of the value of our life and work was in the fact that it was done at the point of the sword."

The new Bishop of Exeter proved to be as supportive of the FSJM as his predecessor. Aware of their difficulties regarding Sunday worship, he found them a resident chaplain, Father Chapman, a priest who needed light duties, as he had been ill with tuberculosis. Unfortunately, Chapman was not sufficiently recovered and left after only a year. His successor as chaplain, the Revd Sir Patrick Ferguson-Davie, a tall, rangy aristocrat, proved to be a much greater success. Ferguson-Davie did not live-in at Posbury, as he had other duties as honorary chaplain to Bishop Mortimer and, as 5th Baronet of Creedy, the management of Creedy Park, an estate four miles to the north of Posbury. Nevertheless, he came to Posbury to say Mass for the Sisters twice during the week and every Sunday.

In addition to taking the services, Father Patrick provided another valuable service to the community. The ordination retreats, which took place from Tuesday to Friday before the ordination service on Sunday, were a fairly intensive experience. Each day there would be three or four addresses and the ordinands were expected to maintain silence throughout the day apart from during breakfast and the evening meal. On Saturday, they went for a rehearsal at the cathedral, after which they were invited by Sir Patrick to Creedy Park. Here, at his sizeable Jacobean-style mansion, built in the early twentieth century after the original house was destroyed by fire, they could let off steam before the solemnities of the next day; enjoying the extensive landscape gardens or joining in with increasingly hilarious sing-alongs around the grand piano.

As the war drew to a close, a growing number of guests were received at Posbury. In addition to those on retreat, many came for short breaks, as post-war travel restrictions meant journeys further afield were limited. Post-war rationing was also still in place, and this led to a difficult moral dilemma for the Sisters. Milk was fetched daily from the farm at the foot of the drive, where the farmer was happy to turn a blind eye if they exceeded their ration. However, when he made it clear to the Sisters that they should not betray him if questioned by the authorities, they realized they needed to make alternative arrangements. Consequently, Sister Mary and Sister Bride were despatched to Cannington Agricultural College in Somerset for a short course in dairy management. In December 1947, two Jersey cows, Stella and Gemma, came to Posbury, to be joined by Angela in April 1948. It was now possible for the Sisters to provide all the milk, butter and cheese required for their visitors without breaking the law.

As with the domestic animals, Mother Teresa considered the cows to be part of the community, noting in a Christmas newsletter: "All the lesser brethren are flourishing. The cows had a wreath of holly and evergreens at Christmas to decorate their house, and each one hung up a stocking for the reception of an extra ration of hay and turnips."

The lives of the "lesser brethren" continued to be documented in great detail in the newsletters: a white cat, Josie, was described peacefully sleeping in the Christmas crib adjacent to the "Bambino", while the latest dog, Brother Angelo, was noted to be very devout due to the number of times he attended Office in the chapel. When Angelo eventually died, he was buried behind the crucifix in the burial ground with the Sisters reciting the Benedictus. At the time, this Franciscan attitude to animals would have been considered by some to be at best anthropomorphic and at worst blasphemous.

Devotion to the teachings of their patron saint could sometimes raise difficult dilemmas for the Sisters. Mother related the problematic situation of a fox, which had built an earth near to their poultry house:

> It was with real sorrow and a sense of shame that we all went down to the woodland to cut and clear away all the cover of bracken and brambles which made it possible for him to have his home so close to the house. For it is certainly one of the results of the Fall that we cannot allow him to live so near to us, and it is we and not Brother Fox, who are to blame.

During the ten years following the war, Mother Teresa oversaw a considerable number of projects as, through trial and error, the nature and work of the community began to take shape. The buildings at Posbury continued to evolve, beginning with the refurbishment of the chapel in 1947. The bedroom over the sacristy, originally accommodation for a stable lad, was removed, allowing the low ceiling in the chapel to be raised and providing space for a gallery which could be used by the Sisters when there were large numbers at worship. The house opposite St Luke's Chapel, Lord's Meadow, which had provided overflow accommodation during retreats, was ultimately deemed unsatisfactory due to its separation from the other community buildings. Mother Teresa wished to build sleeping quarters for the Sisters within the grounds with the proceeds of the Lord's Meadow sale, instructing their architect, Stanley Natusch, to draw up plans. He designed a rectangular building of two storeys projecting north on the higher ground behind the chapel, which could be accessed from the "bridge" which joined the main house to the chapel.

The plans were duly sent to the government offices in Bristol for the required permissions, as building works were still subject to post-war restrictions. The application was refused, but with the recommendation to re-submit a specification without the use of controlled materials. Mother's response was to demand an interview. She journeyed to Bristol with Sister Mary and, after a lengthy meeting with a junior official, submitted an amended application for ten cells rather than the original 12, with a flat roof and concrete construction to avoid the use of timber, one of the controlled materials. After this was also turned down Mother wrote to the head of department in uncompromising terms, saying: "We could not accept the refusal to let us build after having been promised it, and that the building was necessary for the expansion of our work, and asking for the name of the final authority." Permission for the amended application was swiftly granted.

Work began in late spring 1950, and in September the new building was blessed by the bishop. Followed by a procession of 70 people, he moved from cell to cell, each named after saints chosen by the Sisters, sprinkling them with holy water. After the ceremony, the extension was set apart as an enclosed space, entered only by the Sisters when their own cells were occupied during retreats. The building was christened Nazareth, as its white walls and flat roof gave it a passing similarity to buildings in the Middle East.

By spring 1951, their chaplain, Father Patrick, had become increasingly concerned that Teresa was pushing herself too hard and should take a break. He and his wife Iris were planning a pilgrimage to Assisi, and he suggested Teresa should join them with another Sister as companion. Mother, perhaps recalling the restlessness that had taken her younger self to America, chose Sister Hilary, whom she felt might also be inclined to similar feelings, having joined the community at such a young age. The pilgrimage was a great success. The young Sister Hilary kept a diary, which she later typed up and pasted into a scrapbook with a collection of photographs and postcards. The experience of visiting the great Franciscan pilgrimage sites—the Basilica of St Francis, the Carceri and San Damiano—are recorded in great detail and with a sense of wonder. So also is the landscape and, rather touchingly, the meals—as guests of the Revd Sir Patrick they were travelling in some style. Recalling her first meal on the Blue Train which took them from Calais to Rome, she wrote: "We had soup, then some kind of cold sausage, watermelon, vegetable mayonnaise and sardines, following hard on one another so that at one time we had melon and sardines on the same plate. Then we had veal, potatoes the size of marbles, baked in fat, and haricot beans in the pod. After this rolls and cheese followed by pears—one good dinner!"

During their visit, they spent three days with the Larks of St Francis, where they were greeted "like long-lost friends", before finishing their trip with visits to Florence and Siena. Thereafter, pilgrimages to Assisi, whenever funds would allow, became an important element in the life of the FSJM. In Italy, they could reconnect with the sites so redolent of their patron saint and also with the group of Italian Sisters whose unconventional community life had been so influential in the formation of their own. It was also a chance to bring back physical mementoes, such as plaques, figurines, seeds and cuttings, to beautify Posbury.

In 1952, Teresa travelled to St Hilary to meet up with old friends. While she was there, she was distressed to see that the stone altars, which had formed an integral part of Bernard Walke's reordering of the church, were now in the churchyard in various states of disrepair. The only undamaged one, the altar from the Lady Chapel, she decided should be removed to the grounds at Posbury, for the saying of Mass during the summer months. Permission for its removal was sought and granted by Dr Hunkin, the Bishop of Truro and the Chancellor of Truro Diocese.

The Sisters chose a site on the eastern boundary of the main lawn close to a magnificent cedar of Lebanon and set the altar within an arched construction built by Sisters Hilary and Mary from red sandstone carried down from the old quarry at Posbury Clump. On the wall behind the altar, they set a copy of a Della Robbia plaque depicting the Virgin in adoration of the baby Jesus, brought back from Italy. The altar was blessed and dedicated to Our Lady of the Angels and St Francis by the Bishop of Exeter on a typical English summer day in July 1953, amidst squalls of rain, with the bishop protected from the elements by Father Patrick's umbrella. And so, the celebration of Mass at the outside altar, against a background of trees and flowers with the accompaniment of birdsong, became a fixed part of the summer schedule at Posbury. Elements of nature were incorporated into the religious ceremony, such as the strewing of flower petals and the inclusion of domestic pets in the congregation.

Following the earlier success at Meeth, in 1950 Teresa set out with Sister Hilary on a mission to the village of Harberton in the South Hams. Ever creative, Mother had secured, free-of-charge, a caravan for her and Sister Hilary to stay in, from the manager of a local caravan park.

Although the mission was hampered by a lack of co-operation from the local priest, they were a big hit with the local children, who enjoyed the novelty of attending Morning Prayer in a caravan before going to school. Other external projects during this period included short services on the wards at the hospital in Exeter and an ecumenical collaboration with the Roman Catholic Bridgettine nuns at South Brent on the southern edge of Dartmoor.

In 1952, prompted by another donation from one of the Sisters, the community embarked on their sole attempt at a capital project outside their small estate. They decided to buy a house in St Thomas, one of the poorer districts of Exeter, where they had a good relationship with the parish priest. At 165 Cowick Street, a small townhouse situated on a busy street close to St Thomas Church, they planned to provide after-school care for the many "latchkey" children whose parents did not finish work until long after the end of the school day. Situated between two public houses, the Turk's Head and the Moreton Inn, the house had a large bay window at street level into which the Sisters put pictures, an open Bible and an invitation to enter. The children who answered the request were organized into groups for play, handiwork and religious instruction. There was an oratory at the top of the house where prayers were said, before the children were sent home. Despite a certain amount of unruly and disruptive behaviour, Mother Teresa was delighted to observe they were reaching children from the most deprived backgrounds: "We had a group of boys coming regularly who went to no church or Sunday school and several were police court cases on probation, but they were fond of us and we of them and their visits to us certainly meant something to them." In February 1953, 23 of the St Thomas children came to Posbury for a party, and in April three boys and three girls were baptized. However, as the numbers coming to retreats at Posbury increased, the Sisters began to struggle with their workload, and in 1954, on the advice of their warden, Father John, they made the regretful decision to end the St Thomas project.

Shortly after the Cowick Street house was sold, Priestcott, the five-bedroom house which had formed part of the original Posbury estate, came on the market for the third time since the original auction. Teresa had long wanted to incorporate the building into the community, but the previous times the house had been on the market she lacked sufficient funds for the purchase. Now, however, they had money in the bank. The newly acquired house was rechristened St Mary of the Angels, after the basilica in Assisi where St Francis received his calling to the religious life. Rather than utilizing the building as extra accommodation for retreatants, the Sisters decided on a new initiative: holidays for deprived children. Two Extern Sisters had indicated that they would be interested in running the enterprise, but the project was not to prove a success. After only one unsuccessful year, Mother observed of the women: "They were not co-operative and the children who stayed in the house did not like them or settle happily with them at all."

Eight years on from the construction of the gallery, the chapel accommodation was beginning once again to feel cramped, as the numbers attending retreats and Quiet Days continued to grow. One of the Sisters received a legacy in 1955 and, in accordance with the unwritten rule of the order that the community should not hold funds, the Sisters decided to use the windfall to extend the chapel with the construction of a new aisle on its northern side to form a Lady Chapel. Stanley Natusch drew plans for a space that could seat 24 and also an adjacent room with a bathroom for the use of the priests and any other men staying in the house. This required digging out the bank which sloped upwards adjacent to the chapel, a task which took three weeks due to persistent rain. The Sisters became concerned the costs might exceed the legacy, but were reassured by Natusch they need not worry. Accordingly, he reduced his fees and paid in part for the massive cylindrical stone pillar which divided the new aisle from the main body of the chapel. Behind the altar at the head of the aisle Natusch incorporated a niche to hold a statue of the Virgin, similar to ones the Sisters had seen in Italy.

Continuing the continental theme, they had a bellcote constructed which housed a ship's bell given to them by a priest friend, Theodore Sharpe. Every morning at Mass its single note sounded the Angelus across the valley, redolent of the bells that rang out over Assisi. There were no funds left for seating and, in a move that would horrify conservationists today, Father Hooper provided a set of 400-year-old pews from his church at Kenn. The chapel was then dedicated rather than consecrated.

This was on the advice of the bishop in case the Sisters ever needed to sell Posbury.

In tandem with the development of the built fabric at Posbury, despite the limited workforce, was the continuing restoration of the gardens, including the development of the market garden. Mother observed ruefully: "Dame Nature is still very much able to show us 'where we get off', in spite of all our talk about 'conquering nature'." The combination of Sister Mary's expertise and Mother's vision saw the grounds undergo a significant transformation. The lines and features of the ornamental garden were now once more discernible: on the eastern side of the main lawn, a long herbaceous border; on the western side, terraces of mown grass cut into the sloping land, bordered by shrubs and surmounted by a line of trees; to the south-east of the lawn, amongst the sloping woodland, a series of ponds were fed by a spring and planted with water lilies and aquatic plants. To these features, the horticulturalist Sister Mary added a rock garden with Alpine blooms close to the house, lending variety to the traditional English garden favourites in the main borders. A yellow climbing rose grew up the elegant wrought iron columns into the curvilinear brackets of the Regency veranda and specimen trees and shrubs were planted against the wall of the chapel.

In the wider estate landscape, Teresa reported in the February newsletter that finally the saplings and undergrowth had been cleared in Posbury Clump, to provide areas for quiet contemplation:

> There is so little solitude in our bustling noisy world, we think the greatest treasure we can offer to share with our brethren is the silence and the peace in which Posbury is enfolded, for it is in silence that Our Lord speaks to our poor distracted souls.

Despite this conscious cultivation of a place apart, a literal retreat from modern life, the Sisters in their prayer life and intercessions were fully tuned into the challenges facing the post-war world. Sister Margaret listened to the news each day, after which the Sisters hung cards with relevant prayers on Wilhelm's candleholder in the chapel. At the outbreak of the Korean War, Teresa wrote in the August 1950 newsletter:

> It may appear to some that we do not seem to be interested in affairs outside our small domain, but it is not so! There is little one can say or write about the opening again of the abyss of war beneath our feet, except that it is not to be wondered at, seeing how far the world has travelled from a spiritual conception of life and its purpose.

She was appalled by the threat of nuclear war and wrote in March 1955 of her dismay that Great Britain had chosen to have the hydrogen bomb as part of our arsenal. Later in the same year she observed:

> This freedom that we share with other countries, is ringed round with fear and shadowed and conditioned by H. bombs and all the rest of the fearful armoury behind which we take cover, telling each other that these weapons are the necessary bulwarks of our peace and freedom. I wonder do any of us really believe these grim modern fairy tales?

The Sisters were increasingly concerned about reports emerging from Russia with regard to the treatment there of Christians. During the war, attendance at Russian Orthodox church services had been tolerated, but under Khrushchev in the late 1950s a new anti-religious campaign began, leading to the persecution of Christians and the confiscation of church property.[1] Rather than condemning the country as a whole, the Sisters sought the merciful intervention of God. Mother urged those who read the newsletter to pray for Russia, observing the Sisters said the prayer "saviour of the world, save Russia" every day after vespers.

More joyful national events were also observed. In the May 1953 newsletter, Teresa reported the Sisters would be praying for the Queen on her coronation, noting a month later with splendid self-assurance: "And it is so good and helpful to our prayers for her, to remember always that our Queen is also our sister, a younger sister to many of us, in that life of sacrament and prayer which we all share as members of Christ's Mystical Body, the Church."

On 16 July 1955, Teresa and Sister Margaret celebrated the silver jubilee of their taking their first vows; they were 66 and 62 years old respectively. As Mother considered this date to be the founding date of the FSJM, they made sure the occasion was suitably marked with a Mass at the garden altar sung by the Bishop of Exeter in front of a congregation of around a hundred people. Notable among the guests was their former prisoner of war Wilhelm Jacobs, who had travelled from Germany for the occasion with his wife Teresa and was given the honour of carrying the processional cross.

As 1955 closed, Mother reflected on a year in which 240 people other than the Sisters had slept at Posbury. She also observed the readership of the newsletter was now so widespread it extended not just throughout the country, but also to medics working in a leprosy centre in Uganda, to a group of women in the parish of St John, Ilaro in Nigeria, and to two teachers and a nurse who were working elsewhere in Africa. Despite having achieved so much and being well past the national age of retirement for women, Mother Teresa gave no indication she had any plans to step back from her duties.

Notes

[1] Lyubov Soskovets, Sergei Krasilnikov and Dina Mymrina, "Persecution of believers as a systemic feature of the Soviet regime", *SHS Web of Conferences* 28, 01098 (2016), <DOI: 10.1051/shsconf/20162801098>, accessed 18 July 2024.

CHAPTER 13

A change of rule

In 1956, the Bishop of Exeter approached Teresa with the request she provide the community with a written rule and statutes. He assured her he had no issues with the order while she was its leader, but knew a clear guide was needed for whoever was ultimately to succeed her. The bishop's concern was understandable, as Teresa was now 68, with a heart condition. In her memoir, she confessed to having avoided the task "because of an inner fear of legislation that is binding on either people or circumstances". Curiously, she makes no mention of a previous constitution and rule she wrote which was signed by Bishop Curzon on 27 June 1935, the day she and Sister Margaret took their full vows.

The updated version was an extension of the earlier rule with greater detail, specific reference to the buildings at Posbury and a statement of the principles and daily practice of the community. Significantly, specific reference is also made to the appointment of the Mother: "The Mother will be elected for a period of seven years, and may be re-elected for a second period, but must retire after fourteen years as Mother." After two months of drafting and re-drafting, in consultation with her fellow Sisters, the final version was sent to the bishop. He in turn consulted with their warden, Father John Hooper, before the rule and statutes were submitted to the Advisory Council for the Religious Communities. The document received full approval, with Father O'Brien SSJE informing the bishop: "It was a pleasure to read a document so clear and unambiguous in its contents ... sane and balanced and a help towards forming Franciscan vocations."

Despite this enthusiastic reception, the nonconformist in Teresa continued to question the formality and the constrictions the rule implied. Four years later, in the 1960 October newsletter, she wrote eloquently about the rule and rules of religious orders in general:

> We must realize that the spirit is above and beyond the rule. The function of the rule—the letter—in any society, is to be a pointer and guide, and at times a coercive support to our constantly wavering and rebelling minds and wills. And by our obedient submission to the rules of the Church and of a religious community or fraternity, we arm ourselves against the weakness and foolishness of our mortal state, yet must be aware that the most meticulous keeping of a rule is not of itself alone creative of the spirit which gives life.

Meanwhile the development of Posbury as a place of retreat, in a setting of exceptional natural beauty underpinned by prayer and conducive to contemplation and spiritual renewal, was now reaching its maturity. Teresa's newsletters contain lyrical descriptions of the gardens: "It is a joy to both eye and mind to stand on the veranda and look down the garden where dahlias and sunflowers, Michaelmas daisies and gladioli, stand in the glow of the sun"; the wider landscape: "The little wood is beautiful now with masses of primroses and violets, and the wild cherry blossom is making a soft cloud of white against the blue sky overhead and the sharp green foliage of trees in their first leafing"; and the abundance of wildlife: "Swifts and sparrows have been building nests in the thatch and swallows in the garage."

Those experiencing this Franciscan haven were many and varied—from a mother and her five children who sought a temporary refuge from a troubled home at Priestcott in 1956, to the university students who came each summer from Exeter College, Oxford, bringing their welcome energy and enthusiasm to chores about the house and gardens. Teresa's unconventional version of the religious life attracted young people who might otherwise have felt intimidated by more conventional orders. In 1958, Exeter University held its first retreat for undergraduates at Posbury, and among their number was a geography student, June Roberts, who later joined the FSJM as an Extern.

One of the most well-known figures to enjoy the seclusion of the Sisters' Devon retreat was the anti-apartheid campaigner Father Trevor Huddleston CGA. For many years, he and Teresa had been corresponding before finally, in 1958, he came to lead a retreat for the Sisters. Huddleston was back in England after 16 years in South Africa and had recently published his hugely influential book *Naught for Your Comfort*, a cry of anguish over the injustices of apartheid. Over the years, he was to return twice more: briefly in Easter Week 1963 when he was visiting England as Bishop of Masasi and again in 1973 to lead a further retreat for the Sisters after he had been made Bishop of Stepney. These were private visits for the benefit of the Sisters alone.

In 1957, Father Edward Pizey came to Posbury as live-in chaplain. At 77, he had had a varied ministry including two years as a mission priest in Australia, 15 years as the incumbent at Walkhampton on the western edge of Dartmoor, and a final ministry at St Silas, Pentonville. Like Father Hooper, Father Pizey was an Anglo-Catholic celibate who had known the Sisters from their early years at Posbury, when he paid for the stained-glass window depicting St Francis in the chapel. He was apparently undaunted at the prospect of occupying a cramped room off the staircase to the gallery above the chapel and soon became a familiar figure around the lanes riding his motorbike. Father Hooper continued as warden after he moved to the Diocese of Oxford in 1959 as Vicar of St Mary Magdalene, the Anglo-Catholic parish church at the heart of the university and town.

—

It must have been a source of some frustration to Teresa and the Sisters when projects had to be abandoned, not because they were unsuccessful, but because they simply did not have the womanpower to keep them going. Just as they had regretfully turned the key for the last time on 165 Cowick Street, they concluded in 1958 that, after ten successful years of cow-husbandry, they could no longer maintain their small herd. Mother wrote eloquently in April 1961:

> The one great and crying need which we have to struggle against, until it is fulfilled, is the lack of fresh vocations to our life. The work grows incessantly and without seeking on our part—we have often to refuse rather than seek opportunities which come our way, because we have practically reached the point where we

> can do no more ... I know that many of our friends do pray for vocations for us, but perhaps not always with the realization of the difficulties and the precariousness of our way of life which must increase unless we have more Sisters in the next few years, and indeed as soon as possible!

Despite the inexorable demands of Posbury life, Mother made sure time was allowed for the spiritual and physical rejuvenation of the Sisters through pilgrimage and retreats. In May 1960, she accompanied Sister Mary on a pilgrimage to Fulda to visit the relic of St Boniface before journeying to Oberammergau to see the Passion Play.

From the mid-1950s, the island of Iona became a destination to which Teresa would retreat for rest and to gain perspective on life at Posbury. On returning for the first time in 1956, she described renewing her spiritual friendship with St Columba: "I have always been drawn to the saints of the Celtic Church, who seem to have had, among their many graces and attractions, the same loving, reverent joy in the natural creation, and an intimate kinship with animals and birds, as had St Francis."

The Sisters had another place of sanctuary, an equally idyllic location on the cliffs above Porthcurno in the far west of Cornwall. The Haven was not much to look at—a tiny two-room corrugated iron chalet with a galley kitchen, one cold water tap and a privy in the garden—but its view looking straight out to sea with the white sandy beach below was arrestingly beautiful. Their accommodation came free-of-charge courtesy of the redoubtable Rowena Cade, who had bought the headland on which The Haven perched in the 1920s, and later built the famous open-air theatre at Minack. Five years younger than Teresa, Rowena was undoubtedly a kindred spirit, cut from the same cloth: both were women of vision with determination to see their projects through to completion, whatever the cost. The Sisters would visit frequently, usually in pairs, for rest and recuperation.

In August 1962, Patricia Millington, a 20-year-old from Nottinghamshire, came to Posbury to test her vocation. Although young, Patricia already had a great deal of life experience—after attending art college she worked as a nanny for a wealthy family, during which time she received a marriage proposal from her employer's younger brother. However, an increasing sense of vocation drove her to leave her comfortable post, and the even more comfortable prospect of marriage to a man of means, to work as a nursing assistant. She considered becoming a Franciscan tertiary, before a chance encounter with a woman who had previously tested her vocation at Posbury encouraged Patricia to visit.

On arriving at Posbury, she was welcomed enthusiastically by the Sisters. Slight of build, with arresting dark eyes, she had an engaging demeanour, which combined poise with spontaneous merriment. The sincerity of her faith and utter acceptance of the requirements of poverty, chastity and obedience persuaded Teresa she was a suitable candidate for the order. For her part, the future Sister Agnes was equally enchanted:

> I loved my new life, and I remember for weeks going impatiently to bed each night with a longing for the next, and the next, new morning to break. To break and be gone and to hasten on towards that wonderful day when I was to be clothed as a novice.[1]

Towards the end of the 1950s and into the early 1960s, the newsletters made increasing reference to Teresa's health problems and her need to take breaks away from the strain of running the order. Although aware of her advancing age and decreasing physical vigour, it nonetheless came as something of a bolt from the blue to those outside the community when, in the newsletter of February 1963, she announced that on 4 March she would be stepping down as Mother. Details were given of the process for finding her replacement:

> We shall hold an Election Chapter on that day, and on the next day, we shall have a Quiet Day under the guidance of our Warden. On the 6th, during a Sung Mass at 9 am, the Bishop of Exeter, who is our Visitor as well as our dear friend, will install the new Mother, giving her through his authority, the blessing and authority of the Church to rule and guide the Community. This will be a day for which I have prayed, and to which I have increasingly looked forward for several years.

Teresa noted that the community itself had been preparing for this eventuality for 15 months and that she would continue to hold the title Mother, as she was the foundress of the order, and would still write the newsletter—clearly, she was not yet ready to give up this significant conduit between the Sisters and their wider community of friends and supporters.

The following newsletter in March 1963 revealed the new Mother, who was to be known as Reverend Mother to distinguish her from Mother Teresa. Many of those outside the community had been expecting Sister Mary to be chosen. She had many attributes eminently suitable for the role, including intelligence, eloquence and a natural air of authority. At 46 years old, she was still very fit with the potential for many years of active leadership. However, the surprise result of the election, which Teresa described as unanimous, was the elevation of the youngest full member of the community, Sister Hilary, to the role of Reverend Mother.

The reasons for this decision were various, and in some respects can only be the subject of speculation. Sister Elizabeth later indicated to her nephew, Martin Shaw,* that the Sisters whose manual labour underpinned the smooth running of the community—herself, Sister Faith and Sister Bride—desired a less authoritarian leader who might bring some youthful informality to her leadership style. It is likely that the elderly Sisters, Margaret and Bernadine, would have been influenced by Teresa's views, who in turn may have thought she could mould the new Mother; harder to do with an older woman. Teresa may also have felt a certain kinship and affinity with the young woman she had known since she was a girl and who, like her, had the disadvantage of being born illegitimate. Her announcement in the newsletter focused on the merits of the new incumbent's youth:

> This is a great joy, especially perhaps for me, because she came to us very young, and just after we arrived at Posbury St Francis, twenty-one years ago. So, she has seen all the development and expansion of our life here, and although she is the youngest in age of the professed Sisters, she made her final vows in 1949. It is

---

* Later to become Bishop Martin Shaw, the final Visitor to the FSJM.

good for us to have a young Mother now, for as one grows older and more tired, one is less adventurous in spirit and might not be very willing to hear the word as it was spoken by God to the Israelites, "speak to the children of Israel that they go forward", and that could be a disaster!

Another factor may have been Sister Mary's lead role in the management of the garden and concern she might have struggled to continue this while also carrying out the duties of Mother. And so it was that the shy and diffident Mother Hilary, who at 36 years old had already lived more than half her life at Posbury, became the second Mother for the FSJM.

In May 1963, Patricia was clothed as a novice and took the name Sister Agnes, chosen for her, as were all the Sisters' religious names, by Teresa.[*] Despite her diminutive height she brought youthful vigour to her work in the garden, learning quickly under the exacting tutelage of Sister Mary. She had a natural facility with children and proved a good public speaker. She progressed smoothly through her training, taking her simple vows in March 1966 and, in July 1969, just three years after joining the order, her life vows. Teresa described the event:

> It began as always with us with the Community going in procession up to the Chapel from out-of-doors, singing as we went, 'O happy band of Pilgrims', Mother Hilary led the young Sister carrying her bouquet and the rest of us followed after including the Extern Sisters who were with us for the occasion.

—

The need to raise funds was an ongoing concern. In October 1962, the community held their first Open Day, beginning with a Mass in honour of St Francis at the garden altar. Guests were encouraged to bring a picnic lunch taken on the front lawn, before browsing stalls selling Christmas cards and crafts, followed by afternoon tea. Around 300 people attended,

---

[*] As with Mother Hilary, the name chosen for the young novice referenced the early years of Teresa's journey to found the FSJM.

including coach parties from Torquay and Plymouth, and the event made £147. Such was its success the Open Day became an annual fixture, attracting increasing numbers and providing a regular source of revenue. By 1974, attendance had risen to over 400, raising £405.

In addition to substantial running costs, considerable investment was required in the maintenance and repair of an historic building. Consequently, in 1963 the Sisters took the decision to reroof the main building in slate as the cost at c.£1,500 would prove lower than the regular spend required for repairing and replacing the thatch. Teresa lamented the impact on the charm of the building—the tall brick chimneys, originally required to prevent sparks from igniting the thatch, now appeared rather etiolated in contrast to the uniform greyness of the new slate roof. Thatch, however, was a luxury they could not afford, and when the chapel and then the adjoining priests' quarters needed attention, they too were reroofed with slate and tiles respectively.

Another major and unseen cost came in the autumn of 1970, when the spring which had provided water throughout the Sisters' time at Posbury failed and they were faced with the cost of laying pipes to the mains water supply in the adjacent hamlet. Incredibly, all these expenses were met through the Open Days and vigorous fundraising.

An important contribution towards the maintenance and repair of the house and grounds was the input of voluntary workers. In addition to the regular help from undergraduates, annual working parties came from poor parishes in the West Midlands—initially in 1966 from Sedgley and from 1970 onwards from Ocker Hill near Tipton. They were brought by Father John Howe when he was curate at Sedgley and later parish priest at Ocker Hill. As an undergraduate at Exeter College, Oxford, Howe had been among the student party who came to Posbury in 1958 and was consequently aware of the importance outside help played in its maintenance. He would also have seen the pastoral opportunity for his city-pent parishioners for whom a holiday in the countryside would have been beyond many of their means. The relationship with the West Midlands parishes had a satisfying reciprocity: the parishioners travelled to Devon by coach to spend a holiday free-of-charge with fresh home-cooked food in a glorious rural setting and in return spent their days painting, constructing outbuildings, sewing and gardening. Whole families came to stay, and for the weeks of their visits there must have been an atmosphere of cheerful, noisy industry. The families were recruited from their local churches and in October 1971 Sisters Mary, Bernadine and Agnes held the first of several missions back there.

Teresa stepped back further from community life in September 1967 when she received permission from their warden and the community chapter to move into Priestcott (which she always referred to as The Angels) to live in semi-retirement with Sister Margaret. Both women were in declining health and from then on only joined their fellow Sisters for Mass (and on special occasions for Vespers), recreation and meals.

Meanwhile Mother Hilary continued her predecessor's commitment to ecumenism. The FSJM maintained their contact with the Roman Catholic Bridgettine Order in South Brent, visiting them twice a year, and the newsletter was sent to three different Roman Catholic orders. In 1966, Sister Mary attended an ecumenical retreat at Clewer, and in 1972 the Sisters hosted separate groups of Baptists, Methodists and Roman Catholic Franciscan tertiaries.

Under Mother Hilary's leadership, the FSJM stayed true to Teresa's original vision of a community open to the wider world. The peak of this contact came in 1965 when the Sisters featured in a BBC television programme which aired a few days before Christmas. On Mothering Sunday in 1972, Sister Mary was invited to preach on the religious life at evensong in Exeter Cathedral as part of a special Lenten series in which four of the preachers were women. On a more local scale, the Sisters further strengthened their ties to the community in 1974 by starting a Sunday school for the children of the parish.

The retreats, Quiet Days, conferences and working parties attracted increasing numbers. Between the mid-1950s and the mid-1970s, there were on average 15 retreats each year, with *c.*300 people staying in the house and *c.*1,000 visiting the community in total. Teresa wrote in May 1959:

> To provide a place of spiritual peace, along with the loveliness of garden and countryside which is still comparatively untouched by the haste and bustle, and the feverish rush from one thing and place to another—seems to us to be one of the really important aspects of our vocation.

In order to maintain this atmosphere while hosting large numbers, times of silence and the regime of prayer were strictly maintained. Every Friday continuous silent prayer for those in particular need in the world was said in the chapel from 9 a.m. until the evening meal.

In December 1970, Jean Salter came to Posbury to test her vocation. Twelve years previously, when working as a receptionist at a doctors' surgery, she met Mother Teresa and Sister Bernadine during a mission they conducted at her local parish church in Paignton. Jean found Mother Teresa inspirational, but did not feel free to join the Sisters, as she was the sole carer for her elderly mother. She did, however, become an Extern and made regular retreats to Posbury until she was finally able to join the Sisters, following her mother's death. After six months as a postulant, on 7 June 1971, she received the habit and took the name Sister Giovanna. Mother Teresa described the ceremony in detail in the July newsletter:

> The Clothing is a simple ceremony, beginning with the entrance into the Chapel of the postulant at the same time as the priests and servers. She carries in her hands a bundle consisting of her habit and cord, and this is placed by the Altar till the time for its blessing. As the procession comes in it is our custom to sing the hymn "Jesus calls us o'er the tumult of our life's wild, restless sea", when a novice is received into the Community. At the Offertory of the mass, the postulant makes her request to be admitted to the Community and also her promise of obedience during the period of her novitiate. The habit is blessed and the postulant goes out of the Chapel to be clothed in it. On her return, a prayer is said in which her new name is announced.

Despite the wait, Sister Giovanna was still only in her late 30s when she joined the order and was immediately deputed to assist Sister Mary, along with Sister Agnes, in the garden. Sister Bernadine also benefitted from Sister Giovanna's help in the sacristy, as she was already familiar with the duties from her church in Paignton. In April 1974, Sister Giovanna made her simple vows in a ceremony during which the scapular and cord were added to her habit along with a silver ring.* Father Hooper returned to Posbury to preach at the service, his role as warden by this point having passed to Father John Tate, a former sub-warden of the Community of Mary the Virgin, Wantage.

The muddy Devon country roads had eventually proved too much for the redoubtable Father Pizey and his motorcycle, and in March 1965 he left for full retirement in Exeter. His successor, Father Cecil Gault, a recently retired military chaplain, had been a friend of the order for 17 years. Despite having an austere no-nonsense disposition, he baulked at the primitive priests' accommodation adjacent to the chapel and offered to build a bungalow at his own expense within the grounds. With the Sisters' agreement, and with military efficiency, Merrymeet (named after a convergence of two tracks on the boundary of the Posbury estate) was built on the site of a former tennis court to the south-west of the main house.

In 1973, Bishop Robert Mortimer announced his retirement. The news was met with great sadness by the FSJM, as he had been a great supporter of the community, as had Mrs Mortimer, who had become a friend to the Sisters. She would visit them regularly to help with tasks such as needlework and with preparations for the Open Day. Bishop Mortimer's successor, Bishop Eric Mercer, was very different in disposition, being far less academic and much more "down to earth",† but he proved to be an equally supportive visitor.

In many respects, the life of the FSJM at Posbury during the 1960s and 70s followed the model created by Mother Teresa, with its round of retreats, Quiet Days and an Open Day at St Francistide. However, in other ways life under Mother Hilary's leadership differed significantly. On taking up her new role she did not relinquish her duties in the kitchen and most mornings would be found there presiding over the vast Aga. Here she prepared lunch (or dinner as it was known), which was the main meal of the day, assisted by Sister Bride. Only in the afternoon would she take her place in Teresa's former office; a long, thin room with a canted bay which retained the diamond-leaded windows from

---

* Sisters received gold rings when they made their full vows.
† The words used on his memorial stone in Exeter Cathedral.

the original design of the *cottage orné*. She was assisted in keeping the accounts by Sister Faith, who many years earlier had been a bookkeeper in South Africa. The office was strategically placed at the opposite end of the main corridor from the front door, giving the occupant immediate sight of any visitor entering the house. Teresa had relished being at the heart of operations; in contrast, Mother Hilary was more comfortable and self-confident in the kitchen.

From the outset, Teresa had run Posbury as if it was an impoverished minor stately home. Although the rooms were sparsely furnished, with items gleaned from friends and charity shops, they were carefully arranged and always beautifully maintained. The stone passageways on the ground floor were rigorously swept, the wooden furniture polished, and the soft furnishings regularly laundered and mended. Fresh flowers were placed in every room, including the cells. Although the household chores continued to take place under Mother Hilary, the ambiance in the house underwent a significant change. She did not share Teresa's highly developed aesthetic sense, instead adopting a more utilitarian approach to running the household. Clutter began to build up, with boxes piled in corridors and unwieldy stacks of paperwork materializing in her office.

When she stood down as head of the order, Teresa had continued with the two tasks of instructing novices and writing the newsletter. However, as she moved into her mid-80s, she reluctantly made the decision to hand over these duties to her successor. In January 1974, she wrote in her 352nd newsletter: "And now I have to tell you that this is the last *Newsletter* I shall write. Changes have to come, perhaps we have too many of them now-a-days, but this is one that I think is right."

This decision signified the end of an era. Her newsletters, described by Father Gault as remarkable for their spiritual depth, were also full of comment on the issues of the times. She condemned the Vietnam War: "It is utterly wrong and can by no means be squared with the faith professed by Christians of any denomination"; was sceptical of the space programme: "There is something rather pathetic about the eagerness for exploration and conquest of other worlds, in a race which fails so signally in the right understanding and management of the planet on which we live!"; lamented the killing of Martin Luther King: "The world lost perhaps its most wholly Christian and valiant warrior for Christ and His oppressed black children ... It would indeed be well for us in England if we had one such Christian leader as Martin Luther King"; and was intrigued by the hippy communes: "it is a step in the right direction, to desire and seek for a way of life removed from the fierce competition in which so many people have to live against their will, and to seek to share what one has with others."

In addition to sharing her thoughts on current events, through the newsletters Teresa continued to campaign for the issues she had promoted throughout her life: prisoner welfare and the rehabilitation of offenders; pacifism and subsequently the campaign for nuclear disarmament; the anti-apartheid movement and environmentalism. She also advocated the traditional Christian values she felt were becoming lost in the modern world. Despite being a pioneer in the cause for the emancipation of women, she was adamant the role of women was distinct from that of men:

> It is still true and always will be so, that the primary vocation of woman is to build and conserve; to guide and influence the world and its plans and policies through the God-given power of moulding and shaping character, which is inherent in her person. This is the greatness of women; they may reach the heights of intellectual achievement and business success, but their essential dignity and greatness lies always in this particular quality of spiritual power which works from within, holding and bearing with Blessed Mary, the knowledge and experience of both the joy and the sword of the vocation of womanhood.

She was equally firm on the importance of church buildings:

> Our churches should be places of refuge for us, we do not really need to be amused or entertained in them, but we do need and can usually find the stillness which comes through prayer and adoration. It is inspiring and comforting to remember when one can pray in an ancient church, that the very walls are impregnated with the prayer of centuries, for the joys and griefs, the humble

penitence and loving offerings of a countless number of souls have been sanctified within them.

Mother Hilary took over writing the newsletters from February 1974—although Teresa would still make contributions from time to time following significant events. Father Gault remarked of Mother Hilary's writing: "She was good, yet not a match."* Rather than emulate the style of her predecessor, who would begin with either a homily relating current events to scripture or a meditation on the lives of the saints, Mother Hilary stuck to relating news of the life of the FSJM. Her letters were tremendously informative but lacked a spiritual dimension. When she felt this was required, she would quote extensively from Teresa's thoughts in previous newsletters.

Her approach to training postulants also differed radically from her predecessor, who had constantly sought and appealed for new members to join the FSJM. Mother Hilary saw the time required to guide a postulant into a radically new way of life as a demand too far in an already overloaded schedule. Teresa's aspiration that a younger Mother would take the community forward with an adventurousness of spirit was becoming increasingly unrealistic.

Assuming leadership from Teresa, the founder of the FSJM, was always going to be extremely difficult. In addition to the practical skills required was the need to win hearts and minds while having the confidence to take things forward in new directions. When she took over as head of the FSJM, Mother Hilary had the advantage of both youth and experience of the community at Posbury, having joined the order at such an early age. The latter, however, was two-edged as she had limited education and little life experience outside the order. Additionally, all the Sisters, from Sister Margaret to Sister Giovanna, had joined the order partly in response to the personal charisma of Teresa—she was a hard act for anyone to follow.

As already noted, one of the clauses included in the rule written by Teresa in 1956 prescribed a fixed period of office for the Reverend Mother

---

* Remark made in a conversation with Michael Blain, one of his former parishioners who stayed with Father Gault at Posbury when training for the priesthood at Mirfield.

of seven years, with a further seven following a successful re-election, before retirement after 14 years. An election duly took place after Mother Hilary's first term of office with the Sisters casting their votes in a secret ballot. However, the result, revealing a unanimous win for Sister Mary, was met by a stunned silence, after which Mother Hilary, Teresa and Sister Mary swept from the room for a private discussion. It transpired Sister Mary was dismayed by the result and adamant she would not accept the role. Consequently, Mother Hilary remained in office and the vote, which had proved so upsetting and unsettling to the community, was never repeated.

Notes

[1] Sister Agnes, *A Tide that Sings* (London: SPCK, 1988), p. 72.

CHAPTER 14

End of an era

In 1973, 53 years after the founding of the FSJM, the community experienced its first death when Sister Bernadine suffered a fatal stroke on 8 August. It came without warning and was a shock to her fellow Sisters. After Teresa and Sister Margaret, she was the most senior Sister, having shared their journey from the early days in City Road. Her quiet and diligent work, assisting with the housework, weaving habits and acting as sacristan, had provided a vital service to the community.

Through her gifts as a craftswoman, Sister Bernadine had also brought the order a visual identity, decorating many of its official documents with the distinctive symbol *Pax et Bonum*, the crossed arms of Christ and St Francis showing the stigmata. She crafted an official early version of the rule with a punched leatherwork cover and carefully lettered pages and made name cards for each of the Sisters' rooms. Here she allowed her creative talent free rein with a variety of designs. For St Hilary, she chose a stylized design of three ancient books surrounding the name which itself was bisected by a quill. For St Mary Magdalen, the name is surmounted by a very competent copy of Fra Angelico's "Noli me tangere" fresco from San Marco in Florence. For the Sisters' library, dedicated to St Anthony, she made a sensitive copy of the portrait of the saint by the fifteenth-century Venetian artist Alvise Vivarini.

The night Sister Bernadine died her body was taken to the chapel where the Sisters kept a watch of prayer. On the day of her burial, they followed the hearse with their banner to the graveyard where the burial took place.

There were now seven Sisters living in the house, with Teresa and Sister Margaret at "The Angels". Neither was in good health. In 1968, Teresa had undergone another operation, and there were frequent references in the newsletters from then onwards to her and Sister Margaret's various ailments. This did not, however, stop Mother Teresa taking on a new project in 1973, when she began to pay weekly visits to a hostel in Crediton, which she described as "open to receive men who have been in trouble of various sorts—drink, drugs, and prison, but who seem likely to be able to start again after a period of residence in the house". She must have relished a chance to return to one of her favourite causes, the rehabilitation of those she believed suffered from unhappiness, with whom she had always felt a spirit of kinship.

The declining health of the older Sisters, and accidents and illness among the younger members, made the reality of running a small estate, attempting to be virtually self-sufficient and periodically hosting large parties of visitors increasingly challenging. It was a far cry from the life of quiet contemplation associated with the religious life. Coupled with Mother Hilary's reluctance to train postulants, this may explain why no further Sisters joined the order permanently. Although benefitting periodically from the help of Externs, neighbours, annual working parties and the occasional paid employee, the day-to-day running of the community was carried out by the seven younger Sisters, the term "younger" only apposite in distinguishing them from Teresa and Sister Margaret. Sisters Elizabeth and Faith were now entering their 70s, Sisters Mary and Bride were in their late 50s, and Mother Hilary and Sister Giovanna in their late 40s. Only Sister Agnes, in her 30s, was still young and vigorous, but weighing just seven stone she was not perhaps best suited to some of the tasks which inevitably fell to her.

Teresa had firmly believed the integrity of her unconventional religious community required rigorous discipline and order. Mother Hilary had continued the practices of her predecessor, but by the 1970s this strict application of obedience may have been another factor which deterred young women from joining the order. The Sisters' spiritual reading was chosen for them, originally by Teresa and then by Sister Mary. These books were read privately each day in the chapel for an allotted time. Silence was kept at most meals when there were no visitors in the house, during which the Sisters were permitted lighter reading they chose themselves from the common room bookshelves. There was a hierarchy of sleeping quarters with the more senior Sisters having the rooms with sinks and the younger Sisters rotating rooms so as not to become too proprietorial of their own space. Each room was simply furnished with a single bed, chair, chest of drawers, small cupboard and chamber pot. Fasting before morning Mass was strictly observed.

The vow of obedience required no junior member of the order to question the instructions of a senior Sister, even if she could see it was in error, and a Chapter of Faults, took place every Friday. Here the Sisters stood in a circle in the sacristy to confess all the faults of the week, no matter how small: such as banging a door, forgetting to lay a fork at the dinner table or being late for a meal. The Sister would end her list of misdemeanours with the words "and I beg pardon of you all" before bowing and leaving. The exercise would begin with the most junior and continue until only the Reverend Mother was left. The practice of limiting the Sisters' contact with the wider world and current affairs persisted. Each day, Sister Margaret continued to listen to the radio news, enabling the Sisters to compose appropriate prayers for Wilhelm's tenebrae in the chapel. The only newspaper taken was the regional paper the *Western Morning News*, a copy of which arrived once a week.

There were, however, charming elements to the life at Posbury. They lived in such close proximity to nature that wild birds were encouraged to nest, not just in the eaves but within the building itself, and there was the constant presence and companionship of the resident dog and cats. Breakfast was taken on the veranda, except in the most inclement weather, and the beautiful grounds and surrounding countryside were available to explore during their recreation time, allowing the Sisters, like their patron St Francis, to draw on nature as a source of joy and spiritual sustenance. Members of the Sisters' families were permitted not only to visit but also to stay, which enhanced the "family" atmosphere.

Throughout the 1970s, Posbury continued as a popular destination for retreats, conferences and Quiet Days and in spring 1974 received confirmation of its significant place in the life of the diocese when Bishop Eric Mercer chose to hold a staff conference there for two nights. On this occasion, along with their diocesan, the Sisters hosted his two suffragan bishops, the four archdeacons and the Dean of Exeter.

On Easter Monday 1977, Bishop Eric returned to Posbury to say Mass at the profession of the final vows of Sister Giovanna. Teresa, Sister

Margaret, Sister Faith and Sister Elizabeth were unable to attend the ceremony as they were suffering with flu. All the Sisters recovered apart from Sister Margaret, who only a fortnight later was dead. Her Requiem Mass was conducted by Father Gault and, in a tribute to her musical past, the Precentor from Exeter Cathedral played the organ and led the singing.

The May newsletter included a personal tribute to Sister Margaret from Teresa. She praised her friend's wholehearted commitment to the religious life, beginning with her giving away a much-loved grand piano to a struggling young pianist, and paid particular tribute to the role Sister Margaret had played in supporting her in the formation of the FSJM: "we had no clear ideas as to what God wanted us to do here, nor how we should be able to support ourselves. I could not have faced it all alone."

The two women undoubtedly shared a very deep bond of friendship which began with their first rain-soaked meeting in Blisland, when each recognized in the other a soul mate. Their approaches to growing the order perfectly complemented each other, Margaret's quiet resolve acting as a foil to Teresa's fierce determination. Furthermore, for the impecunious Teresa, Margaret's independent financial means were quite literally a Godsend. On a personal level, Teresa was able with Margaret to put aside the persona of Mother, allowing them to share irreverent moments of humour such as their clandestine fast-breaking tea in Paisley, the purchase of the scandalous "wedding cake" and trailing comically around Assisi in each other's cloaks. Even towards the end they shared the dark humour of guessing the date when Margaret would finally die. Mother ended her tribute to Sister Margaret with the words: "In all the fifty years during which we lived and worked and prayed together, she never once failed me."

Sister Margaret's death closely followed the loss of another significant former member of the Posbury community. Father John Hooper died after a heart attack in January 1977. His Requiem Mass took place at St Olave's Church in Exeter, where he had been parish priest in retirement in the early 1970s, following which his body was taken to Posbury for burial. Mother Teresa paid tribute to their former chaplain:

> He always stressed the primacy of the contemplative aspect of our life, often he said to us "You know, it wouldn't matter if you never did any outside work, so long as you go on digging an ever deeper well at Posbury of prayer and adoration". He loved us all, and identified himself with us. It was never to him, "the Sisters at Posbury", but "we at Posbury".

He left his library to the community: an inspiring mix of theology, history and art. Held in high regard in the diocese, an appeal in his memory funded a full set of handcrafted bookshelves which were installed in the priests' sitting room just off the sacristy.

The following year Father Gault retired as chaplain, but continued to live in his bungalow, Merrymeet. After the death of Sister Margaret, Mother Teresa left The Angels (Priestcott) to rejoin her fellow Sisters in the main house, leaving this accommodation free for Father Gault's successor. For the first time, the chaplain at Posbury was a married man, Father Ralph Guild Davison, who moved into The Angels with his wife Esme in September 1978. Many years previously, while he was a priest in the Exeter Diocese, he had written to the Sisters asking them to consider him as a future chaplain. After 14 years ministering in the parish of Ashcombe, Somerset, on his retirement he wrote again to enquire whether he might still be considered for the post. This happened at just the time Father Gault decided to stand down, and the Sisters were delighted to accept someone they already knew, whose love of the countryside and gardening made him a good fit for the community.

Teresa was profoundly affected by the death of Sister Margaret, but her indomitable spirit came to the fore and she rallied, celebrating her 90th birthday in October 1978. Mother Hilary observed in the month before her birthday: "Mother Teresa is marvellous for her age and comes to Mass and Vespers, prays a lot, enjoys seeing the visitors and enjoys the garden when the sun shines and having a break now and again by going to stay with friends. She hopes to go to St Hilary, Cornwall in September, when a stone Altar is to be dedicated in memory of Father Bernard Walke."

Teresa did manage to make the pilgrimage to St Hilary, where she stayed with Canon Leslie Rule Wilson. During the visit, she was reunited with some of her former charges from the Jolly Tinners—Jim Richards and Albert Jenkins. Also present was Emma, Father Bernard Walke's former maid, with whom Teresa had shared the vision of the Virgin of Light and who subsequently joined her at Blisland, before their amicable parting following the grim first years in Paisley. Mother, in elegiac mood, consented to a recorded interview with Canon Leslie about her life and the formation of the FSJM. This account expanded on the memoir she had written eight years previously and a history of the order she had included in the newsletters between February 1969 and February 1970. She clearly felt at ease in Canon Leslie's company—as the tone of the interview is far more candid than the other accounts.

On a further trip to Cornwall, this time to Bude, in November she suffered severe back pain and was taken to hospital in Plymouth. Returning by January 1979, she felt well enough to include a message in the newsletter:

> First of all, my most grateful thanks for all the greetings cards and gifts I received at Christmas, and for the letters of sympathy in my unexpected trouble! You will understand, I cannot hope to answer my letters except in this *Newsletter*. I am recovering slowly, the spine has healed, but I am still in my room only moving to the next room when I am up for several hours. The Family has been marvellous to me—playing lexicon and visiting me in my room—and greatest joy of all, saying the lovely Epiphany Vespers with me, instead of in Chapel.

She concluded her message with the hope of returning to "some sort of normal life", but by Whitsunday her health had again deteriorated and she returned to bed.

On 6 June, she was found on the floor of her room. The doctor was called but concluded she had not had a stroke and would probably recover after a good night's sleep. After administering a tranquilizer, she left her in the hands of one of the Externs, Molly Boxall, who lived locally. Mother Hilary and Molly sat with Teresa until she slept and then Mother Hilary went to the chapel to pray. At 1.10 a.m., Molly rang the house bell and announced Teresa had stopped breathing. Mother Hilary recalled:

Mother had stayed exactly as I had left her and simply stopped breathing, so her soul winged its way in the most peaceful and serene manner. For her it is a great release as her body was becoming a real trial to her while her mind remained clear and active ... She spoke frankly, as many of you will know, of her desire to be released from this life and she always, missed Sister Margaret greatly.

A sung Requiem Mass conducted by the Bishop of Exeter was held for Mother Teresa on 11 June. Eighty-nine people attended the service and followed her coffin, singing in the sunshine, to the graveyard, where the rhododendron hedges were in full bloom. And so the woman who in her youth had been deemed too unfit to train as a nurse died at the venerable age of 90, having realized her vision of creating a new religious order.

CHAPTER 15

Unsustainable loss

Although Teresa's death was felt profoundly by the FSJM, her advanced age meant it had little practical impact on the running of the community. By this point Mother Hilary, still in her early 50s, had 16 years' experience as Reverend Mother, ably supported in her role by Sister Mary, and there appeared to be no existential threat to the FSJM. There were fewer Sisters, some of whom were entering a less active stage of life, but there were still enough, with assistance from friends and the Externs, to keep the community in working order. What was not generally known was that the one person on whom many felt the future development of the community depended had begun to question her vocation to the FSJM.

Unbeknown to her fellow Sisters, Sister Agnes had been wrestling with her response to a profound experience many years earlier on a pilgrimage to Iona in October 1976 with the Extern, Sister Columba—she had received a calling to bring back the religious life to the Isles. Apart from telling Sister Columba, Sister Agnes had kept the experience to herself, although some of her struggle may have been apparent to Sister Margaret who, two days before her death, told the young Sister she and Mother Teresa had always thought Sister Agnes had a vocation to prayer.

The prospect of starting a new life at the other end of the British Isles, far away from the Devon countryside she had come to love, filled Sister Agnes with apprehension. Despite the hard work, she considered life at Posbury in many ways to be idyllic and was fully receptive to the beauty and numinous atmosphere of the place: "Often the day spent, I would stand at the small window of the cell I used, and stare out over the dimpsy colours of a red, green and gold patchwork of rising hills. How those hills drew . . . ."[1] These were productive years for Sister Agnes both within the community and outside it, where she discovered a gift for public speaking. During Lent 1982, she joined her fellow Sisters on a pilgrimage to Assisi, which included a visit to the Larks of St Francis and coincided with a visit from the pope. But the call persisted without a response, causing her conflict and distress. She later recalled: "The timing of God is not as our timing, and a period of seven years, undoubtedly the unhappiest and yet the most formative of my life, was to elapse before the same call was repeated."[2]

The repetition of the call took place in October 1983, when Sister Agnes was staying as the guest of two friends of the community on the island of Fetlar in the Shetlands. She recalled: "That same call had come again, and exactly as I had received it on Iona, though this time a decision had to be made . . . I had made up my mind, and knew for sure and certain and whatever the cost, there could be no going back. My answer was yes."[3]

Her vision was a simple one: a small group of Sisters who would live modestly, following the ideals of the early Franciscans. However, the journey to realizing this vision was to prove almost as arduous as that taken by Teresa. Sister Agnes foresaw there would be a cost to her endeavour but could not have predicted just how high it would be.

On returning to Devon, she decided the right course of action would be to share her intentions with the warden who visited the community every quarter. When, however, it became apparent he would not be coming until the following January, she decided to write to him outlining her plans in detail. She then gave the letter unsealed to Mother Hilary in order that she could read it before it was sent. The seven years of procrastination must have reflected Sister Agnes' trepidation about the reaction of her Reverend Mother to her decision, and her fears turned out to have been well founded. Mother Hilary was at first dismayed and in turn deeply discouraging. She did not share Sister Agnes' intentions with any of the Sisters apart from Sister Mary, who was privately quietly supportive of Agnes. Mother Hilary, however, thought the young Sister was making the wrong decision and rejected out of hand her suggestion that her new order could be an offshoot of the FSJM. Consequently, the two weeks awaiting the arrival of the warden were ones of great anguish for Sister Agnes, confronted, as she was daily, with the hostility of her Reverend Mother.

Once the warden finally arrived, a simple ceremony took place in the chapel, attended only by Sister Agnes, Mother Hilary, the warden and the Bishop of Exeter. During the ceremony, Sister Agnes was released from her obligations to the community and returned the possessions of the order: her copy of the rule and the gold ring given to her when she made her full vows. The bishop then placed on her finger a new ring (her late mother's wedding ring) as a sign that the vow she had made to the religious life still held. Thus, the two senior priests handled beautifully the ceremonial element of her departure. What followed was less satisfactory. Mother Hilary was so upset by the loss of such a key figure in her community that she was unable to handle the situation with generosity.

After the service had taken place and her habit had been returned, Sister Agnes was given clothes from the "ragbag"—a pair of trousers, an army surplus shirt, an anorak and a scarf to tie round her cropped head. The day of her departure, 21 November, was a significant one for the FSJM, as the day they traditionally celebrated the Feast of Our Lady of Light, commemorating the day Teresa had her vision. As was the custom on this day a sung Mass was held in the morning, during which Sister Agnes had been told to sit apart from the Sisters in the gallery. The Sisters then had a celebratory breakfast, but Sister Agnes was told to go to the kitchen, where her breakfast had been laid on a tray. The previous night Mother Hilary had told the other Sisters that Sister Agnes would be leaving, so it was unlikely that many of the FSJM were in the mood for celebration that morning. After her solitary breakfast, Sister Agnes was ordered to her room to await the taxi which would take her to the station. Mother Hilary had made it clear to the Sisters that there was to be no formal farewell, but as Sister Agnes left the house for the final time Sister Elizabeth and Sister Mary, who had been working in the garden and had heard the car as it came down the drive, stood by the gate silently with tears streaming down their faces. And so, after 21 years of community life, Sister Agnes left the FSJM for good.

Sister Giovanna felt her departure keenly, as the two younger Sisters had worked closely together in the garden sharing tasks and jokes—their laughter ringing out over the grounds. On sunny summer days, summoned by the cowbell, they would sit on the steps of the chapel saying the office of Sext—dressed in simple brown dungarees with brown hoods over their white headbands and workman's boots. The incongruous mix of religious devotion and agricultural dress, all set against the picturesque backdrop of an historic rural building, epitomized the very essence of the FSJM. Now, suddenly, an essential component of that special character had been lost. No mention was made in the newsletters. Gradually word got round to the friends and Externs that Sister Agnes had left, but Mother Hilary and Sister Mary refused to discuss the matter further.

—

There were no further permanent additions to the order, but a number continued to join the FSJM as Externs. These included June Roberts, who had first come to Posbury on retreat as a student at Exeter University. In the intervening years, she had become a teacher and on occasion would bring a group of young teenagers to help in the garden; noting the experience had a transformative effect on her more troubled pupils. Not long afterwards Lillian Beveridge became an Extern. She too had a long-standing association with the FSJM, being one of the original group of schoolchildren who attended the Sisters' after-school club in St Thomas, Exeter in the early 1950s.

The receiving of Externs followed a similar pattern to that of the Sisters, albeit with a shorter timescale: a period of probation, followed by a novitiate before taking their full profession. The Externs made a promise, rather than the three monastic vows the Sisters made, which was renewed annually at St Francistide or during a retreat at Posbury—at one point there were 36 Externs, both men and women, in attendance. They all wore the brown scapular with a red cross on the front tied by a white cord with a single knot representing obedience. Originally the women wore white veils, but this practice fell into disuse over time, with only Sister Faith continuing to do so. The Externs were presented with a candle at their profession, which was not to be lit again until their funeral.

In 1984, Mother Hilary proved she was every bit as astute at property developing as her predecessor. Four years previously she had entered into negotiations with Rowena Cade to purchase the small chalet known as The Haven in Porthcurno. Rowena had become good friends with the

Sisters over the years. She was a regular attender at the local church of St Levan and welcomed the addition of a full row of the FSJM when they visited. Consequently, she sold the chalet and adjoining garden to the Sisters for a very reasonable sum. The corrugated iron-clad structure was coming to the end of its natural life. Mother Hilary instructed a local builder, Frank Thomas, to build a new bungalow on the site with the proceeds of the sale of a house in nearby Newlyn, left to the FSJM by two Sisters. The Sisters now had a comfortable place to come to recuperate and let the bungalow between visits to clergy and their families at a low rate.

The year 1986 began badly for the community: Esme Davison, the chaplain's wife, died, and all the Sisters contracted flu. The following year Father Patrick Ferguson-Davie died. Mother Hilary recalled the service he had provided to the Sisters when they did not have a chaplain and how, at his suggestion, they held an Easter Vigil long before the practice became widespread in Anglo-Catholic churches. Father Gault decided in September 1987 that he could no longer manage independent living; he moved into a home and died shortly after. More positively, two Extern Sisters, Sister Mary Woodrow and Sister Vi, came to live in Merrymeet, and earlier that year, in May, there was the golden jubilee of Father Davison's priesting, which included a Mass in the chapel filled to capacity with friends and 25 priests.

In 1987, 22 years after their first visit to Posbury, the BBC returned to film a programme in the series *Through the Garden Gate*. They interviewed a number of the Sisters but, unsurprisingly, Sister Mary was the star of the show. Throughout the programme, she spoke authoritatively both as a horticulturalist and a religious. She explained the ethos behind the garden—based on Teresa's principle of enhancing the beauty of nature without exploiting it—that had led to an environment where the Sisters and visitors alike could commune with God. She described how in the greenhouse the earth was hand-dug and organic and, in the two acres of land under cultivation, everything that she and Sister Giovanna planted was sown with prayer. Her view was reinforced by Mother Hilary, who described the purpose of Posbury as providing a place where people who were stressed could relax.

The programme also showed how the decline in numbers was affecting the community. Though still viable, Mother Hilary conceded the Sisters could no longer spend much time on the ornamental garden, having to concentrate on growing fruit and vegetables. Sister Mary observed she did not know what would happen in the future, but put her trust in God's hands, and overall the Sisters gave a very positive picture of community life. Sister Giovanna reflected that at Posbury she had found religion, work and friendship and had enjoyed every minute of her life there. Towards the end of the programme, Sister Mary stated she had no regrets about her decision to join the order and found the life most fulfilling. The programme was broadcast on BBC South West in March 1988 and the following year was shown on the national network, resulting in increasing visitors at the Garden Open Days.

In 1984, the Sisters had featured in the book *Unknown Devon*, which told stories of obscure aspects of life in the county. The Posbury section included a history of the house, a description of the Sisters' daily lives and an appreciation of the garden:

> The rhododendrons are as high as trees and there are camellias and mahonia japonica, abutillons and clianthus puniceus—also called lobster's claws or parrot's bill—and cowslips rescued from a Cornish building site. Lawns stretch down below the house to the water garden and woodland garden, and beyond stretches a glade where in the last century the gentry held summer evening parties.[4]

Four years later they featured again in *Changing Devon*, a book describing the "rich tapestry of modern Devon",[5] illustrated with engaging and at times elegiac black and white pictures by the photographer Chris Chapman. The article appeared at the end of the book, with Sister Mary reiterating her uncertainty about what might lie ahead for the order when asked what the future holds. She responds: "I don't know at all. The Lord hasn't made it clear to us that he wants us to change and do something else and until he does there's no point in making plans."[6]

One further brush with celebrity occurred at some point in the 1980s when the Sisters were visited by the comedian and broadcaster

Sir Harry Secombe. Oddly, Mother Hilary made no mention of this in her newsletters, but the event was recorded by a photograph, later made into a postcard, in which Sister Mary sits on her tractor with Mother Hilary and Sir Harry to one side and Sister Giovanna with their dog, Max, on the other.

During the BBC programme, Sister Mary gave some interesting statistics about the FSJM, noting that over the summer around 400 people would come to Posbury and up to 2,000 would drop in during the course of the year. As the years passed, it became apparent that Posbury, like the religious sites the FSJM periodically visited, had become a place of pilgrimage and personal significance for a wide number of people. Mother Hilary noted that, during a visit from local schoolchildren as part of their Domesday project in 1985: "One child shyly told us, her father and mother had told her we prayed a great deal for her when she was a baby and critically ill, another that she had been christened in our Chapel, and a boy said his mother had stayed with us after an illness." In the same year, among the three coachloads of visitors to the open garden day was a woman who had lived in a hut in the woods below Posbury with her husband, a charcoal burner, during the Second World War when the Sisters had recently arrived. In June 1989, the Sisters were presented with a cheque for £50 from the local women's branch of Toc H who were celebrating their golden anniversary and 47 years of association with Posbury. That same year at the Open Day a man sought out Mother Hilary to tell her that, as a small boy in the mid-1940s, he had attended woodwork classes taught by Sister Faith.

Many of the clergy who came to preach at the Open Day service had known the Sisters from their time as ordinands, if not earlier. In 1985, John Richards, now Archdeacon of Exeter, preached to 250 people in Crediton Church. He had received a severe reprimand from Mother Teresa on his ordination retreat for breaking the Grand Silence after morning Mass, a witness to the scene observing that at that moment Mother Teresa was every inch the former policewoman! In 1990, the preacher was the Revd Christopher Benson, who had first encountered the Sisters as a young man attending a retreat with servers from the parish of St Gabriel in Plymouth.

The Sisters had always stayed in close contact with their friends and family, and in October 1988, Sister Elizabeth was granted permission to travel to Paisley with her nephew Martin Shaw, now precentor and canon residentiary at St Edmundsbury Cathedral, to attend the dedication of a window in Paisley Abbey commissioned in memory of Sister Elizabeth's brother who had died a few years earlier. While she was away, she suffered a heart attack and died a few days later on 30 October. The family, who had travelled to Scotland for a joyous celebration, ended up attending her Requiem Mass at Holy Trinity, Paisley: the church where she was baptized and where she later met Mother Teresa and Sister Margaret. A Requiem Mass was held simultaneously at Posbury, after which her ashes were brought back for interment in the burial ground in a ceremony attended by 50 of her friends and family.

Two years later, Sister Faith, now 87, was admitted to a nursing home. The Sisters chose St Vincent's, a home at Plympton St Maurice run by the Anglican order of the Sisters of Charity. Sister Faith, with her gentle manner and sweet smile, swiftly became one of their most popular patients. There were now only four Sisters left at Posbury: Sisters Mary and Bride, who were 73 and 78 respectively, Mother Hilary and Sister Giovanna. The diminishing numbers inevitably reduced the number of retreats: in 1981 there were 15, by 1991 only six. However, there were still two Garden Open Days a year and no diminution in the numbers attending the Open Day at St Francistide, with Mother Hilary recording around 300 attending the service in 1981 and the same number in 1991. At the beginning of the 1990s, although very small, the community could still be considered viable.

When Bishop Eric Mercer retired as Bishop of Exeter in 1985, Mother Hilary wrote to him requesting he continue as their visitor. He wrote a charming reply voicing his thanks for the offer but pointing out it would not be appropriate for him to take on a role which his successor might be expected to fulfil. Posbury continued to play its role in the life of the Diocese of Exeter as the venue for the ordinands' retreat and for the Dean and Chapter's quarterly away days.

Following the death of Mother Teresa, Sister Mary's husbandry of the order became as significant as her husbandry of the land. As a popular public speaker, she was one of the FSJM's most effective ambassadors—giving talks, sometimes several times a week, to groups ranging from small Mothers' Union gatherings to a packed congregation at Exeter Cathedral. She was a committed supporter of the Campaign for Nuclear Disarmament and cut a distinctive figure at rallies holding her banner with the unequivocal message: "They that live by the bomb shall perish by the bomb." The role of training novices had fallen to her after Mother Teresa's death, and she became Mother Hilary's trusted advisor.

It was therefore of great concern to the Sisters when, during Christmas 1989, she began to suffer severe pain in her upper leg, caused by the failure of the artificial hip she had been given 16 years previously, and for most of 1990 she was unable to carry out her usual tasks in the garden. Mother Hilary commented tellingly on the strain this had put on the order in the December newsletter: "She was able to give us much needed advice but as it often happens, most things went wrong when she was not here!" She went on to describe how they managed: "Retreatants helped by doing jobs they could do silently, like mopping passages, washing up and the priests in retreat split wood for us and cut hedges and many other jobs."

The episode is witness to the key role Sister Mary played in the order and how her fellow Sisters struggled in her absence.

Following surgery, Sister Mary eventually returned to her former duties, but in July 1993 was rushed to the Royal Devon and Exeter Hospital in Exeter with a ruptured aneurysm. She contracted pneumonia and remained in a deep coma for over a month before finally dying on 28 September.

Her funeral took place on 6 October in the chapel at Posbury attended by friends, neighbours and members of her family. John Thurmer, the Canon Chancellor of Exeter Cathedral, conducted the service. His address paid tribute to her many accomplishments:

> The garden, which has fed and delighted Sisters, guests and retreatants over the years, never ceased to be her interest and concern, and she remained a professional keeping herself up-to-date with horticultural developments. If, in this she was in the spirit of St Francis and anticipated the modern environmentalists, it was by no means her only gift or activity. She drove Teresa and

the other Sisters on speaking engagements, and in due time, took on this work herself. Many priests and lay-people will be recalling the blessings they received from a retreat she conducted or an address she gave.

The rain, which had poured down during the service, abated as the procession left the chapel for the burial ground. It was testament to Sister Mary's popularity and stature that over 250 people attended her memorial service held a month later on All Saints' Day at Crediton Church.

Mother Hilary felt her loss keenly. Although her arrival at Posbury had predated Sister Mary's by a year, such was the latter's competence and authority that Mother Hilary had instinctively turned to her for advice, guidance and support. Sister Mary had been essential to the effective running of the FSJM, and with her death it was inevitable the community was set on a path of decline.

Notes

[1] Sister Agnes, *A Tide that Sings*, p. 75.
[2] Mother Mary Agnes, *Island Song* (London: Triangle SPCK, 2001), p. 19.
[3] Sister Agnes, *A Tide that Sings*, p. 113.
[4] R. A. Lauder, M. Williams and M. Wyatt, *Unknown Devon* (St Teath: Bossiney Books, 1984), p. 68.
[5] J. Derounian, C. Smith and C. Chapman, *Changing Devon* (Padstow: Tabb House Ltd, 1988), back cover.
[6] J. Derounian, C. Smith and C. Chapman, *Changing Devon*, p. 106.

CHAPTER 16

Sister Death

After the death of Sister Mary, life at Posbury initially continued with some degree of continuity. In her nursing home, Sister Faith was no longer part of the community, but with three resident religious—Mother Hilary, Sister Bride and Sister Giovanna—the order could still be considered sustainable. The number of retreats had fallen to four, but with two Garden Open Days, the main Open Day in St Francistide, quarterly Cathedral Chapter away days and a number of Quiet Days, the FSJM remained an important part of both diocesan life and the local community. Mother Hilary was able to observe in the March 1995 newsletter: "We have a good many Quiet Days booked for groups and some retreats, but having lowered the numbers we can manage, the latter are almost full."

Another enduring aspect of Posbury life, albeit continuing in a very reduced form, was the annual visit of the working party from the West Midlands. During summer 1995, four members of the original party repaired the veranda glass, carried out various sewing jobs and prepared vegetables for meals and storage. Mother Hilary observed: "They are pensioners now but very willing and able to do useful jobs which cost quite a lot if done professionally ... We have been very grateful for this help and from our local friends who come for a day a week, or part of one, or for jobs like dropping or lifting potatoes." This enabled Sister Giovanna and Sister Bride, when she was free from her household duties, to continue to work the vegetable garden and the well-established fruit beds. In 1995, Mother Hilary noted a particularly abundant harvest of strawberries, gooseberries, loganberries, redcurrants, whitecurrants, raspberries, mulberries, blackberries and plums. More assistance came from Sister Mary's nephew, who visited Posbury annually from his home in Essex to clear the ponds and prune the trees and shrubs. These included a group of pink azaleas bought with money given in Sister Mary's memory by one of her former gardening pupils, the *Davidia involucrata* (the handkerchief tree), one of Sister Mary's prized specimen trees, and a Cyprus by the back gate grown from a cone brought back from Assisi in the 1950s.

Superficially, the Open Day in 1995 appeared unchanged from previous years. The well-attended service at Crediton Church was followed by a cheerful picnic lunch on the lawn where groups of families and friends caught up with the people they met each year. Children ran through the grounds playing hide-and-seek in the woods while searching for the various Posbury cats and Max. Lunch was followed by the traditional sale with stalls of plants, crafts, puzzles, jumble, greetings cards and sacks of potatoes sold from the tractor shed. Next came the raffle, then a traditional Devon tea of considerable dimensions and finally Benediction at the garden altar. The celebration of High Church traditions within a convivial domestic setting was the quintessence of the FSJM, timeless and endearing. In comparison to earlier years, however, the majority in Posbury brown were not in the full habit but dressed in the belted tabard of the Extern. And the bright stands of Michaelmas daisies, rudbeckia and crocosmia in the autumn borders were tangled with bramble and luxuriantly flowering weeds. Notwithstanding these intimations of decline, the number of people for whom the Open Day was a fixed date in their diaries ensured it was a financial success, with the final proceeds making £2,136.45.

Presiding at the Open Day service that year was the Bishop of Ebbsfleet, John Richards—the former Archdeacon of Exeter who had been a friend and supporter of the Sisters throughout his ministry. The post of Bishop of Ebbsfleet had been created, following the vote to ordain women to the priesthood in 1992, to serve those members of the Anglican community, predominantly Anglo-Catholics, who could not support the decision. The issue had been debated in the General Synod for many years and as early as 1987 Mother Hilary made an unequivocal statement in response to queries about the FSJM's position:

> We are not in agreement with this at all for a number of reasons, the main one being that the Church of England is breaking with tradition... I do not wish to be involved in correspondence over this, only to make our position plain, that we, as a Community are against such a step.

In August 1993, she doubled down on this stance: "We maintain our position, nothing has changed for us, and we have felt all along, if changes must be made, it is those who wish for them who should leave the Church of England." Consequently, following the vote, the Sisters felt they were no longer in communion with their diocesan bishop and took the decision to ask the Bishop of Ebbsfleet to become their visitor.*

A month after the Open Day in 1995, at the age of 91, Sister Faith died in the nursing home at Plympton St Maurice. In the potted history of her life Mother Hilary shared in the December newsletter, she described the tragic circumstances that had first brought Sister Faith to the FSJM:

> She came to England from South Africa in 1935, after the death of her husband, four months before their child was born, and after the death of their little girl at six or seven years old, which were terrible tragedies for her. She believed she would find God's purpose for the rest of her life and found it with our Community when they were in City Road, London, so was given the name Faith.

Her ashes were brought back to Posbury, where they were interred following a Requiem Mass in the chapel.

A year later, another Requiem Mass took place, this time for Sister Bride, who had died on 16 December following a stroke. She was 84 years old. The service was again conducted by Canon Thurmer, who recalled in his address her early involvement with the community as a child in Paisley. He then eloquently summarized the invaluable role she played

---

* In contrast, the Society of Our Lady of the Isles, the community on the island of Fetlar founded by Sister Agnes, now Mother Mary Agnes, voted to accept the ordination of women. Mother Mary Agnes was later to be ordained.

during her 51 years with the FSJM: "She was as much a part of Posbury as the Chapel or the Garden. Stolid, downright, and loyal, living the life of prayer and work, year in, year out, eventually becoming a little slower and more infirm. But she lived the life and did the work up to the last day, disposing of the business of dying within one night-time, as though it were a pity to waste good daylight hours on such a thing."

So, at the start of 1997 the FSJM consisted of just two residentiary members—Mother Hilary and Sister Giovanna. At this point, the general practice among more conventional religious orders would be for the community to close and the remaining Sisters to return to the motherhouse or join another order. There was a recent precedent for this in Devon where the remaining members of the Sisters of the Community of the Compassion of Jesus at West Ogwell had left to join a community in Windsor. Earlier, in the late 1980s, the last two Sisters from the convent of St Wilfrid's in Exeter had moved into a small flat in the city. It was generally assumed that the maintenance of the house and grounds at Posbury, and the obligation to host retreats and Quiet Days, could not be undertaken by two women who were now pensioners and so they too would choose to follow a similar course.

Accordingly, their visitor, Bishop John, never one to shy away from a difficult conversation and with the practical approach of a former archdeacon, consulted Mother Hilary to find out what were her plans for the future. Her response was brief and uncompromising—they would continue as before.

And that is exactly what they did for the next 15 years. Inevitably, this resulted in a gradual and then marked decline in the condition of the buildings. In the grounds, the delicate balance Sister Mary had created between cultivation and nature began to tip away from the former to the latter. The size of the market garden decreased, and undergrowth and weeds once again obscured the ornamental features which had been revealed 60 years earlier. Inside the house, the unused bedrooms lay empty, each single bed with its pile of folded blankets, pillows and eiderdown lying in redundant readiness for postulants who did not come. Over the years, as it became apparent the rooms would never again be used for this purpose, they became storage for items unsold at the Open Day. Piles of books, boxes of puzzles and stacks of Christmas cards accumulated while strategically placed buckets appeared as the roof started to leak and rooms became unkempt, as the Sisters concentrated their housework on the areas still in service. Nazareth, the accommodation formerly used by the Sisters when the house was full of retreatants, was shut up, and it was not long before damp and mould made the rooms totally unusable.

Yet the kitchen with its Aga and comfortable armchair, in which a cat could inevitably be found curled up asleep, still retained its welcoming and cheerful atmosphere. And, during retreats and Quiet Days, the downstairs rooms offered areas of hospitality through the help of the Externs and their friends. The quantities of crockery and china required for catering at scale were brought into service from the scullery, where they were neatly stacked on shelves in a bright blue dresser, apparently repurposed from a former door, which still bore the legend "Chapel". Amongst the motley collection of souvenir ware from churches and resorts and mismatched teacups were charming pieces of majolica brought back from their trips to Assisi. On exceptionally cold days the fire in the recreation room would be lit from wood chopped and stacked by fitter members of the visiting clergy. The creeping decline of Posbury was thus mitigated for the majority of visitors.

—

Towards the end of 1997, Extern Sister Vi moved out of the bungalow Merrymeet to live in a village closer to Exeter, and her place was taken by Father Andrew Rowe, a friend of Father Davison. He was a welcome addition to the small community, as he was a driver and was also willing to take over the duties at St Luke's which were proving too much of a strain for Father Davison, who was now 85 years old. Mother Hilary observed tartly in the April 1998 newsletter: "Many of the folk round about thought he [Father Davison] must be retiring all together, not realizing he was first of all our Chaplain and St Luke's was an extra, not the reverse."

One of the great strengths of Mother Hilary's newsletters was the detailed information she would share about the lives of those associated with the FSJM, be they Sister, priest, Extern or lay person. In the September 2002 newsletter, she wrote in detail about the life of their warden Canon

John Howe, who had celebrated 40 years in the priesthood, including his first experience of the order: "He came to Posbury in 1958 with Canon Eric Kemp, later Bishop of Chichester, and a group of students from Exeter College, Oxford to work in this parish, and there they stayed for ten days, after which Father John changed course and went to St Stephen's House, Oxford, to train for the Ordination and to the Priesthood." In this way, she maintained a real sense of community amongst the disparate people who had been involved with the Sisters, some of them throughout their lives. In 2002, Father Davison died, Father Rowe took over the role of chaplain, and the house at Priestcott was let to tenants. Another loss occurred in November 2003, when their visitor, Bishop John, died suddenly. Again Mother Hilary shared a number of details of his life in her newsletter, reminiscing on their final encounter: "We are most grateful for his friendship and all he did for us, and for the fact that he spent an hour with us a few days before his passing, meeting a young farmer who called and they had a good conversation about the present conditions, the latter when leaving saying 'I hope I shall meet him again. I wish there were more people like him.'"

Now, the newsletters began to catalogue those aspects of life at Posbury which were becoming a burden. In September 2000, Mother Hilary noted they were finding the bees difficult, but hoped to get help from the British Beekeepers Association. The only animals remaining on the site, apart from the cats (Max had joined the departed Sisters in the burial ground), were the hens, looked after by Sister Giovanna. Mother Hilary observed of the garden in 2001: "Although the weeds have overcome us in many places, the flowers of them have been a joy and some grasses too have been extra beautiful, so we have tried to be grateful for the wild and the tame!" Visiting friends continued to assist with tasks such as marmalade making, but the Sisters were finding it increasingly difficult to manage the heavier jobs.

Despite the challenges they faced, Mother Hilary mentioned many of the positive aspects of their lives. On 3 October 1996, she celebrated the golden jubilee of her religious profession with a tea party, followed two years later by Sister Giovanna's silver jubilee celebrations. She described at the beginning of 1998 how the previous Christmas Eve she had listened with Sister Giovanna to a radio broadcast of Bernard Walke's St Hilary nativity:

It took us back to Mother reading the play to us most Christmasses [sic] in the Cornish dialect with its lilting tones and local interpretation. She had helped to produce and dress the earliest performances, so had tales to tell of that, though she had left St Hilary to start the Community, when it was broad-cast first in 1926.

Generous donations from friends also enabled them to continue the Posbury tradition of pilgrimage. They went to Assisi in December 1998, paid for by a friend in memory of Sister Bride; to Bruges in 1999, and then again to Assisi in 2004. To mark the millennium, they celebrated with a Midnight Mass and the following day gave commemorative mugs to a group of local children. Such was the enduring image of the good life at Posbury, the following year they were depicted picking peas as part of a series of photographs taken by Chris Chapman for a permanent exhibition, *A Positive View of the Third Age*.[*]

In 2001, as elsewhere in the countryside, the foot and mouth epidemic seriously impacted life at Posbury. For a period of time, the Sisters were isolated from visiting friends, the footpaths were closed and the Quiet Days cancelled. Garden open days were out of the question, but they managed to do some fundraising at a club in Crediton where they sold bedding plants, preserves and cards. Following this difficult period, the open days recommenced, continuing to be a good source of revenue. The 2003 event, which took place just before the death of Bishop John, raised £2,026.20, paying for the outside of the house to be painted.

It became increasingly apparent, however, that the traditional programme of events—two Garden Open Days, Quiet Days, retreats and the Open Day—was no longer sustainable. In 2005 Mother Hilary wrote:

> We have had to make the decision to have no retreats here this year, for several reasons, and are sorry for this. The few we continued to arrange as our numbers decreased, have not been so well attended, one reason being the increasing age of our regular friends, then the fact that many people find it difficult

---

[*] The exhibition was hung in the Princess Elizabeth Orthopaedic Centre at the Royal Devon and Exeter Hospital.

to keep silence, so go to the modern type, where there is a good deal of sharing and talking amongst the retreatants, or to conferences. We feel this place is more suited to quiet and we, ourselves can serve people much better providing this. Then we have many jobs in the house and garden in arrears which we simply do not accomplish, and we hope having a year free from extra commitments may help us (and our friends) to do so. When retreats are attended only by a few, it is not easy to expect conductors to give their time. We shall not take on anything else this year, excepting to honour one Quiet Day booked a year ago.

She was still not prepared, however, to consider a move to more manageable accommodation. Following the death of Bishop John, ten years elapsed before Bishop Martin Shaw, the nephew of Sister Elizabeth, was chosen to be their new visitor. When he questioned Mother Hilary regarding her future plans, her response was as blunt as the one she had given his predecessor: "We shall die, and we'll go to God. If that's not good enough for you, Martin, I don't know what is!"[1] When sometime later he broached the subject again, her rejoinder was: "Sister Death."

Over the next few years, the community was further depleted when, in 2007, the now aged Father Andrew Rowe left Merrymeet to live in Crediton. For the first time in many years, the Sisters no longer had a chaplain on site. Father Peter Lee, a retired priest from Exeter, agreed to become acting chaplain, taking the service on Sunday and one day during the week.

Community life at Posbury for Mother Hilary and Sister Giovanna now consisted of looking after themselves and those parts of the house and garden they could manage. They continued to hold Garden Open Days and plant sales, although Mother Hilary noted in August 2006: "The garden was very untidy and a wilderness in some places, as everything grows so fast and well, too well we think sometimes." In 2008, she was more positive, noting people had travelled from North Devon, Plymouth and Cornwall to see the garden and observing: "Sister Giovanna still mows the main lawn as it gives her good exercise for her mild diabetes." However, by July 2009 she reported ruefully: "There was much colour from the peonies which were beautiful and handsome even though growing amongst weeds, for so much of our garden is now overgrown."

The Open Day also continued as an annual event and still managed to raise funds. This was now almost entirely due to the efforts of their friends and Externs, although Sister Giovanna still grew plants for the sale, including pots of hyacinth bulbs, and Mother Hilary made jam with the assistance of helpful visitors. The service of Midnight Mass conducted by Father Peter Lee remained popular in the local community.

In reality, the day-to-day running of the community, despite the best efforts of their supporters, was now more than the Sisters could manage. As the number of visitors declined, so the plots in the burial ground increased. In 2006, they interred the ashes of Extern Brother James. In the April newsletter, Mother Hilary recorded: "Jim met Mother and Sister Margaret when they helped in a Mission at his church St Michael's, Handsworth, Birmingham in 1937." He was joined four years later by another long acquaintance of the order, Extern Sister Vi. Incredibly, she had come with the Sisters to Posbury because she was too ill with tuberculosis to work and had then lived until the age of 89.

Mother Hilary herself remained physically strong, but there were signs she was beginning to lose mental capacity. Until 2011, she wrote the newsletter three times a year, but that year there were only two, the second of which, written in December, was shorter than usual and somewhat disjointed. In Easter 2012 she wrote the 511th FSJM newsletter, which was to be the final communication from the order, although it is unclear whether she realized this when she wrote it. It began with the usual greeting, "My dear Externs, Members of the Compassion and Friends", and included the familiar observations on the weather, the significant services they had attended and news of an Open Garden Morning on 9 May. In the second half of the communication, she observed it was 70 years since the community came to Posbury, followed by a number of quotes from Mother Teresa's newsletters in which she describes their early days at the house and the creation of the chapel. The newsletter ends: "So we share our happy and grateful memories with you and ask for your continued prayers, as we pray for you."

The next few months proved difficult as Mother Hilary's illness took hold. This period was hard for Sister Giovanna; having to accept the authority of someone who was losing their mental capacity while bearing the burden of a heavy workload. This came to an end when Mother Hilary was finally admitted to a nursing home in Crediton. Sister Giovanna was now the sole occupant at Posbury. Although she frequently had company during the day, at night she was alone in a large old building which, in addition to the chapel, bathrooms, stores and sculleries, had 34 other rooms. However, solitary living held no fears for her (this was in marked contrast to Mother Hilary, who had always refused to sleep on her own even when staying at the bungalow in Porthcurno).

Following Mother Hilary's departure, an informal group of "trustees" were formed to assist Bishop Martin in his role supporting Sister Giovanna. For a while, they did their best to make Posbury more comfortable, including installing a new bathroom, but it was clear the building was entirely unsuitable for a diabetic octogenarian living on her own. Sister was, however, unwilling to leave her beloved home. Through the kind auspices of her friends, she continued in residence, even managing to host the annual Open Days, initially attended by Mother Hilary, until she became too unwell.

On 9 February 2019, at the age of 92, Mother Hilary died. Her Requiem Mass took place on 12 March at the Church of the Holy Cross, Crediton. It was a day of torrential rain, which continued to pour down as the funeral procession entered through the west door. The coffin, rather than bearing the usual formal arrangement of wreath or bouquet, was surmounted by a simple cross, formed from mounded moss studded with primroses and polyanthus; the combination of piety and natural simplicity perfectly representing the character of the FSJM. Immediately behind the coffin, in her brown habit and cloak, walked the frail figure of Sister Giovanna, accompanying her Reverend Mother on her final journey. Bishop Martin Shaw officiated, with Extern Sister June Roberts giving the first reading and the acting chaplain of the FSJM, Father Peter Lee, leading the prayers. The service was well attended, with people from the many different stages of the FSJM story, and included the only other surviving Extern, Sister Lillian. Following the Mass, Mother Hilary's body was taken back to Posbury for burial amongst her fellow Sisters. And so, with the death of its second and final Reverend Mother, the Franciscan Servants of Jesus and Mary officially came to an end.

Not long after Mother Hilary's funeral, Sister Giovanna agreed to move out of the main house at Posbury into the former tractor shed, which had been converted into a pleasant one-bedroom bungalow. Here she would sit looking out over the fields to St Luke's, reading and knitting until eventually her declining health necessitated a move into nursing accommodation in Exeter.

Notes

[1] "Mother Hilary FSJM dies aged 92", *Church Times*, 1 March 2019, <https://www.churchtimes.co.uk/articles/2019/1-march/news/uk/uk-news-in-brief>, accessed 8 April 2024.

Epilogue

Now that the life of the FSJM has come to an end, what conclusions can be drawn about the order? It must first be said how remarkable it is that it ever came into existence. Mother Teresa had much to overcome, including her own illegitimacy and impoverished background, and the persistent opposition of numerous clergy. But, despite the power of her vision, her call to found a new type of order was unspecific. She had a strong sense of what the order should not be—enclosed, hierarchical—but was less clear about what form it *should* take. So, pursuing a course of trial and error, typical of her brave and determined character, was, while inevitable, not the easiest path to take. Her willingness to test widely different settings and ministries appeared to her detractors as evidence of her lack of clear objectives, but each supposed misstep could be seen as necessary, without which the creation of Posbury St Francis would not have been possible.

That the FSJM found their permanent home in a tiny hamlet in the middle of the remote Devon countryside is testament to Teresa's vision. She saw through the obvious drawbacks of the building and site, which had reduced Sister Margaret to tears, and refused to be daunted by the work required to realize their potential. Similarly, she did not allow the distance to the nearest parish church to deter her, trusting that having their own chaplain would be achievable. Despite her experiences in Cornwall, she would not allow herself to be discouraged by the West Country suspicion of the incomer. In this respect, she was entirely vindicated, with the support of the surrounding community playing a key role in the longevity of the FSJM.

The unorthodox nature of the order did not ultimately hinder the development of its clearly defined mission and character, reflecting Teresa's willingness and flexibility to adapt to circumstances. Evangelism through mission work in rural communities, something she had envisaged in her early days in Cornwall, became a subordinate element in the life of the FSJM at Posbury. Shortly after their arrival, they adapted their model of mission in response to the serendipitous request to host the diocesan ordination retreat. Having met the challenge, they built on this initial success by maximizing the exceptional natural beauty of the site, rapidly establishing Posbury St Francis as an attractive centre for retreats and Quiet Days.

Crucially, one of Teresa's great gifts was to nurture the talents of those who joined her order, allowing these to inform its nature and development. As the FSJM followed the teachings of St Francis, it inevitably attracted women seeking a life of engagement with nature. Physical labour, referred to by Mother Teresa as "the original spiritual work", became a fundamental element of community life. The fortuitous arrival of Sister Mary with her advanced horticultural knowledge provided the opportunity to take this aspect of their life a stage further. Through her skills the historic ornamental garden was revealed and enhanced, providing an idyllic setting for retreatants and a market garden productive enough to provide fresh fruit and vegetables not only for the community but also for their visitors. And she also gave the FSJM the abiding and striking image of a Sister driving a tractor. The musical, artistic and communicative skills of the other Sisters, combined with their willingness to carry out tasks of heavy labour, all contributed to the distinctive character and success of the community.

Mother Teresa was undoubtedly the cornerstone of the FSJM: the community owed its existence to her great faith and fortitude, all the Sisters who took full vows, to some extent, joined in response to her personal charisma, and the causes and concerns of the order reflected those of her early years as a social welfare campaigner. These characteristics contributed to the success of the order in her lifetime, but dependence on such a single driving force could also be seen as contributing to its eventual decline, though the FSJM outlasted the other female Anglican communities in the county.

It could also be argued that Mother Teresa's vision, and its realization in the community she created, was truly pioneering. Fostering spirituality through nature, championing the environment, campaigning for peace and social justice, self-sufficiency and sustainability, all reflect the agenda of church and society today. Although the community life at Posbury has ended, many of the elements of the FSJM ministry continue. Following the closure of the order, Posbury House and Garden, Priestcott and the majority of the fields were sold and the proceeds used to create the Posbury St Francis Trust (PSFT). The objectives of the new trust reflect those of the FSJM: mission, evangelism and spirituality. Grants for spiritual formation and development are offered to groups and individuals living and working in Devon and an annual lecture is organized on the theme of the causes for which Teresa fought. The Old Tractor Shed at Posbury and The Haven at Porthcurno have become venues for retreats, and the burial ground at Posbury is maintained for deceased members of the FSJM as a place of peace and tranquillity for the public to visit.

And for the thousands of people who came to Posbury over the years there are the memories of a place whose mission its founder so eloquently described:

> The grace which the Posbury family asks, is to be allowed to make by prayer, work and love, in the beauty of the Devon countryside, a place of peace and joy, in which the veil between this world and the new earth which is promised to us, may be transparent enough to reveal in the eyes of all who come, something of the immortal loveliness of that country which is our true home.

Afterword

Dr Bridget Gillard has become a valued and very dear friend of mine over the past few years, despite my having originally met her parents, and maybe even herself, at the FSJM's Open Days whilst she was still a child. Hence, the fact that she got in touch with me when starting to research this book was probably due to her father, the Revd John Richards (later to become the Right Revd John Richards, the first Bishop of Ebbsfleet), having also come to Posbury in his earlier years as one of a group of ordinands for his pre-ordination retreats around the time I joined the community, and whilst Mother Teresa was still in office as our Reverend Mother.

Living in the heart of Devon with her husband Ian, Bridget is wholly qualified to write whatever type of history she might choose and, being a trustee of the Posbury St Francis Trust, she felt increasingly drawn to the story of Grace Costin, later known by her name in religion—the Reverend Mother Teresa, of Jesus, Foundress of the Franciscan Servants of Jesus and Mary. Graduating in the history of art and architecture from the University of London, Bridget gained her MA at Leicester De Montfort University, in architectural building conservation, and finally, did her PhD in Plymouth. She is now the executive secretary of the Devonshire Association.

From the outset, Bridget has trusted me with the privilege of reading through this extremely sincere and candid history of Mother Teresa. Chapter by chapter, her work was executed with honesty and deep consideration, yet has also brought to us a hint of the soul of Mother Teresa, that redoubtable woman whom I understood so much more clearly both towards and at the end of her life, and which obliterated what had perhaps been any of her less lovable, more superficially dominant, traits. Without exception, we all know something of the weaknesses of our own human nature, yet it is those very failings and frailties which to a large extent, and with God's loving patience, help shape the inner persons we are to become.

At Posbury, we were well acquainted with the story of an individual who carried around with him a pocketful of stones, all of which, constantly rubbing up against each other, finally became shiny and smooth, thus portraying the often painful, yet positive, communal aspect of human life which, of course, is no less applicable to the religious life! Indeed, within such a lifestyle as recorded in Bridget's history of Mother, most of us religious, if our vocations are true, expect to grow into God with the hope that, at least, just a few of our rough edges will be rubbed off and polished. Hence, in all fairness to Mother Teresa, that is, the *real* Mother Teresa—she who prayed for so many silent hours in chapel, performed many an act of hidden kindness, and passed on great gems of wisdom, which most folk scurrying around upon the surface of earthly existence would hardly have noticed—she did, in fact, show love and warmth, if only in that strange hidden way of her generation, for hearts in those days were rarely worn upon sleeves!

Undoubtedly, she moulded her community in a way which was often challenging to us comparatively younger ones, and especially so to our present-day twenty-first-century world. For hers was an era of following the pattern of former ages when "would-be saints" were still quite sharply chiselled into shape! Nevertheless, I cannot think that it ever did any of us FSJM Sisters any harm and, who knows, perhaps carried us just a wee bit nearer to God's ultimate goal. Indeed, if seriously sizing Posbury up alongside the more established communities of that period, Mother's ideas for the Franciscan Servants of Jesus and Mary were, in fact, thought to be quite avant-garde.

Nevertheless, and marvellously as Bridget suggests, all the positives and negatives of the Posbury part of the journey were undoubtedly balanced and enhanced by the spiritual beauty of its environment, perhaps I should say, the aura of those 31 acres of exquisite Devonshire countryside surrounding the property, which, during Mother Teresa's administration of the order, and Sister Mary's supervision of the grounds and woodlands, extended its quiet essence into the Sisters' beautiful home, always fragrant with pots of flowers and quiet welcome. And where, towards the end of this period, in August 1962, I also joined the

"Posbury Sisters" at the age of 20, was received as a postulant, clothed as a novice, and over the next few years received into simple and later to life vows—so staying with the Sisters, and sharing their life until I was 41. When receiving "a further call within a call", I was taken onwards to Shetland, with the full blessing of both Mother Teresa and the then Bishop of Exeter, Eric Mercer. Yet, ever in my heart there remained that inspirational quality of Posbury St Francis. That charisma which in the early days, and until Mother Teresa and Sister Margaret's retirement from office, remained intact.

People, even nuns, are such a mix of personality, disposition and outlook that it is easy to see how a strictness of rule, either good or not so good, sometimes amounted to an over-zealousness by any one individual in authority. This was certainly so during those earlier generations of such establishments, an era still savouring of the "Victorian". Nonetheless, by 1962, I remember Mother Teresa correcting me soon after my arrival—regarding my eagerness to "give God my all". "Child", she said, "all *you* have to do as a postulant is to persevere!" I smile still, even laugh, for I distinctly remember my dismay at the thought of endless perseverance—an attribute far less romantic and far harder to achieve than any of my own highfaluting ideas of perfection! Yes, she taught me quite a few valuable, often very necessary lessons, and as time went on with an increasing warmth.

Irrefutably, I have always loved and carried Posbury within my heart, however far away I was, for it was a deep part of my formation. However, there was much of the day-by-day history that was missed, so I have found these latter chapters of Bridget's book especially revealing, since many of the facts were unknown to me, not having lived the life with the FSJM at such close quarters over the past 40-plus years. This lack became particularly poignant in Bridget's inclusion of Sister Bride's death and funeral in her last chapter. Indeed, I thought that Canon Thurmer, whom I had known so well at Posbury, had captured Sister Bride's stature and person, perfectly, in his sermon.

Now, I look forward, hopefully, to meeting them all once more in God's beautiful eternity; to hearing Sister Elizabeth's laughter so full of joy; to seeing Sister Mary's passion for the work she was called to do within the environment; for Mother Hilary's lifelong service; Sister

Bernardine's patience and humility; Sister Giovanna's companionship when helping me clear dykes, cut hedges and fell trees; Sister Faith's stability—ever sturdy as a rock—and Mother Teresa and Sister Margaret's perseverance and huge devotion to God. My gratitude to them all, my one-time fellow travellers, for their faithfulness and love of him who called us.

An hour or so after Mother Teresa died in 1979, I stood by my open cell window, in the Posbury enclosure where we each slept, peering out into the dark countryside during the early hours and in amazement heard for the first and last time of my life the exquisite song of a nightingale! And now, in 2024, I still wonder whether perhaps it might just have been Mother Teresa saying her final, earthly, farewell!

Thank you, Bridget, for all your work and scholarship. Many folk, even in far-flung places, will buy your book, enjoy reading it, and be greatly informed. Thank you also for your most precious friendship to this now elderly hermit, pondering upon, and gradually laying aside, the final episode of her own earthly life's journey.

May our loving God continue to bless the author of this story of the Reverend Mother Teresa FSJM, all those who read it, and all others who, in whatever myriad ways, follow his call.

The Revd Mother Mary Agnes, Hermit
Summer 2024

APPENDIX 1

Members of the Franciscan Servants of Jesus and Mary in life vows

Mother Teresa of Jesus FSJM (Grace Emily Costin)

Born	27 October 1888
Simple vows	16 July 1931
Life vows	27 June 1935
Died	7 June 1979

Sister Margaret of Mary Immaculate FSJM (Margaret Phyllis Pearce)

Born	14 July 1893
Simple vows	16 July 1931
Life vows	27 June 1935
Died	25 April 1977

Sister Bernadine of the Holy Name FSJM (Doris Kathleen Coysh)

Born	22 May 1901
Simple vows	13 March 1937
Life vows	22 April 1942
Died	8 August 1973

Sister Hilary of the Child Jesus FSJM (Dorothy Slade Inskip)

Born	12 June 1926
Simple vows	3 October 1946
Life vows	4 October 1949
Died	2 February 2019

Sister Mary of Our Lady of Sorrows FSJM (Elizabeth Mary Cope)

Born	2 February 1917
Simple vows	8 December 1948
Life vows	8 December 1951
Died	28 September 1993

Sister Mary Bride of the Sacred Heart FSJM (Mary Dock Benson)

Born	1 September 1912
Simple vows	8 December 1948
Life vows	8 December 1951
Died	16 December 1996

Sister Elizabeth of the Holy Family FSJM (Elizabeth Lockhead Shaw)

Born	31 December 1906
Simple vows	10 February 1950
Life vows	2 February 1954
Died	30 October 1988

Sister Agnes of Our Lady of Joy FSJM (Patricia Millington)

Born	11 October 1941
Simple vows	1 March 1966
Life vows	1 July 1969
Left the FSJM	21 November 1982

Sister Giovanna of the Incarnation FSJM (Jean Salter)

Born	31 May 1931
Simple vows	25 April 1974
Life vows	11 April 1977
Died	13 December 2024

—

Sister Faith FSJM (Constance Mary Jenkinson)

Joined the FSJM	4 October 1938
Died	13 November 1995

APPENDIX 2

The Constitution, Statutes and Rules of the Franciscan Servants of Jesus and Mary

Statute 1.

The Name of the Community:
Franciscan Servants of Jesus and Mary.

The Motto and Watchword of the Community:
"Nihil Amanti Impossible."

The Purpose and Objects of the Community:
A life of poverty, prayer and labour under the Religious Vows of Poverty, Chastity and Obedience.

The Common life is to be lived in the spirit of Acts Chap. 2. v.44. "And all that believed were together and had all things in common." And Acts Chap. 4. v.32. "And the multitude of them that believed were of one heart and one soul, neither said any of them that ought of the things which he possessed was his own; but they had all things in common."

After the example of Saint Francis of Assisi, for himself and his followers, the Sisters will seek to live in a spirit and practice of peace and charity, working and praying for the salvation of souls, and seeking to draw the hearts of all with whom they come into contact to the love and service of Jesus Christ and to know and love also His Blessed Mother.

The Community is pledged to the observance and practice of the Mixed Life, giving the chief place always to prayer and contemplation, but offering to others, as request or opportunity arises, the fruit of prayer and contemplation in the active apostolate when asked or inspired to do so.

The form of active apostolate outside the house of the Community in which the Sisters may engage themselves, will be the assistance in parochial and other evangelistic and teaching missions, the giving of devotional and instructional addresses to groups such as Mothers' Union and other societies and guilds, and the conducting of simple evangelistic and teaching missions in villages; never less than two Sisters going together for this purpose, and at the invitation of the parish priest.

They may speak to mixed audiences in Churches and elsewhere, if permission from the Bishop is given for them to do so.

The Community may ask for these permissions in any Diocese in which they may be working, for Sisters who are in either temporary or final Vows, but not for Novices.

The Community will not undertake the care of any institution, nor may the Sisters work other than temporarily in a parish.

The life of prayer, hospitality and labour within the Community house must always be the chief concern of the Community, and other work only undertaken which does not endanger seriously the order and rhythm of the common life.

There will not be a separate house for guests, but they must be received into the family life of the Community, sharing meals and recreations, and work if they desire, with the Sisters unless in retreat.

No fixed charges must be asked by the Community for the entertainment of guests, but voluntary offerings may be received.

At the end of the daily reading of the Statutes or Rule the following prayers should be said.

Antiphon. Christ became for our sakes obedient unto death, even the death of the Cross.
V   I count all things but loss.
R   That I may win Christ, and be found in Him.
Prayer. Almighty God, Who hast given Thine only Son to be unto us both a sacrifice for sin, and also an example of godly life; Give us grace that we may always most thankfully receive that His inestimable benefit, and also daily endeavour ourselves to follow the blessed steps of His most holy life; through the same Jesus Chris our Lord. Amen.

V May the divine assistance remain always with us.
R And with our Father, and absent brethren.
V May the souls of the faithful through the Mercy of God, rest in peace.
R Amen.

Statute 2.
Of Membership in the Community

The Community consists of Sisters who have made Life Profession and are thereby full members, Sisters in Temporary Vows, Novices, Oblate Sisters, and Tertiary Sisters living under renewable vows or promises. Oblate and Tertiary Sisters may be either resident or non-resident. If living in the Community house they will wear the distinctive dress provided for them, and observe the House Rule as well as their own individual devotional Rule. They will take part as fully as possible in the life and work of the Community and share in all its benefits, but may not attend the Community Chapters or have any place or share in the government of the Community.

Statute 3.
Of the Novitiate

Candidates not previously known to the Community will be required to live in the house as Aspirants for from two to four weeks before being received as Postulants.

The Postulancy must be for an unbroken period of from four to six months, or in an exceptional case nine months. Admission to the Postulancy is at the discretion of the Mother and Novice Mistress.

The period of noviceship will be for a minimum of two years, which may be extended if necessary to four years.

Reception to the Habit of a Novice will be at the discretion of the Mother and Novice Mistress.

Statute 4.
Of Temporary Vows

The period of Noviceship will be followed by admission to Temporary Vows. Admission is by election, a two-thirds majority of favourable votes being required.

The Temporary Vows are administered under the declared avowal of a life intention on the part of a novice, and no novice will be admitted to the state of Temporary Vows except with such intention.

The Temporary Vows are taken for a period of three years, which may be extended to four years, and are renewed annually. A Sister in Temporary Vows may retire or may be dismissed at the expiration of the yearly vow. If dismissal or release should become imperative during the course of a year covered by the vow a dispensation should be sought from the Bishop who is the Visitor of the Community.

Sisters in Temporary Vows may be allowed to attend the Chapter Meetings of the Community, with the consent of the full Chapter Sisters, but they will have no right to vote until they have made Life Profession.

The minimum age at which a novice may be received to Temporary Vows will be twenty years.

The Formula of Temporary Vows

I, Sister .... make my Profession and Promise to Almighty God before the whole Company of Heaven, in the presence of you Mother, and you my Sisters, and to you Reverend Father, that I will live in observance of Poverty, Chastity and Obedience, for the next year according to the Rule of this Community.

Statute 5.
Of Final Vows

Sisters in Temporary Vows will be admitted to Perpetual Vows, with the permission and consent of the Visitor and a two-thirds majority of favourable votes of the Sisters in Life Vows. The Vows taken are Perpetual Simple Vows administered and taken with an intention of life-long obligation on the part of both the Community and the Sister.

Every Sister in Perpetual Vows is entitled to a seat and voice in the Chapter of the Community. Also to a vote unless she has been for less than six months in Perpetual Vows when an occasion for voting in Chapter occurs.

The minimum age at which a Sister may be received to Perpetual Vows in the Community shall be twenty-three.

Formula of Perpetual Vows
In the name of the Most Holy and Undivided Trinity, and in honour of the Sacred Heart of Jesus and the glorious Ever-Virgin Mary Mother of God: I Sister ...... make my Vow to God to live in perpetual Chastity, Obedience and Poverty.

I offer and consecrate to Him my person and my life, and I give myself up wholly to His Divine Love, to spend and be spent in His Holy Service.

I choose Jesus my Saviour and my God to be the sole object of my devotion. I place myself under the protection and beg the prayers of His Holy Mother, Blessed Mary Ever-Virgin, and of Saint Francis and all the Saints.

And I choose the Society of the Franciscan Servants of Jesus and Mary to be the Community in which I am to devote my life. Glory be to the Father, and to the Son and to the Holy Ghost. Amen.

Statute 6.
Of the Mother

The Mother will be elected by the Chapter, a clear majority of votes will be required. The Mother will be elected for a period of seven years, and may be re-elected for a second period, but must retire after fourteen years as Mother.

The same Sister may be elected again after being out of Office for a period of seven years.

If there should be no Sisters suitable for election to the Office of Mother, when the Mother in Office has completed fourteen years, the consent of the Visitor must be obtained for her continuance in the office for a further period of seven years.

The title of Superior will not be used by the Mother at any time.

The Mother elected will choose her own officers, who may be changed if necessary during her period of office, and they will automatically retire with her at the end of her term of office.

Statute 7.
Of the Chapter

The Community is governed by its Chapter. There shall be an annual meeting of the Chapter of the Community during St Francistide i.e. between the 17th of September and the 11th October. Every Sister in Perpetual Vows shall be a member of the Chapter. An agenda shall be circulated one week before the annual chapter meeting to the Visitor, Warden and Sisters.

Every Sister may send in subjects for the agenda to the Mother not later than ten days before the meeting of the Chapter.

A Special Chapter will be summoned should the need arise at any other time. The presence of the Warden is required of necessity if the election of a Mother is taking place.

The Mother is bound to bring to the decision of the Chapter signified by votes the following matters.

The election of a novice to Temporary Vows, and of a Sister in Temporary Vows to Perpetual Vows.

The setting up of a group of Sisters in a new place and work, any expansion of premises or work which will involve the Community in heavy expenditure: i.e. a sum exceeding fifty pounds, having regard to the poverty of the Community.

Any matter which might imperil the fundamental objects of the Community Life, and any proposed changes to the Constitution or Rule of Life.

A careful record of the acts and decisions of the Chapter must be kept.

Statute 8.
Of Property

The property of the Community consists of two houses, and their surrounding grounds at Posbury St Francis, the furniture, farm animals and implements of work, and such monies as may be either in the house or the bank at any given time.

The Community may not have money invested in its name in any industrial profit-making concern. There may be an ordinary banking account as a convenient place of deposit for any money the Community may have, but no interest bearing forms of deposit may be used.

Any sister having private means or landed property must make a Will before her Final Profession. She will be under no obligation to bequeath all she has to the Community, but must provide for her maintenance within the Community if able to do so.

The Community must be careful not to influence a Sister in her decision as to the disposal of money or other property, but whatever may be donated for the support of a Sister or as a gift to the Community may not be in the form of investments.

After the reception of the habit no one may retain the administration of landed property or private funds in her own hands.

The property of the Community is held in the name of the Mother and two other Sisters in Life Vows who together act as trustees for the Community.

The Community will not under any circumstances take out a mortgage or accept any other form of loan on which interest must be paid, nor will the Community at any time go to Law to obtain or keep possession of money, and or any other goods.

As the Community is small, it is realised that some one or other of the disasters which hang over the world may make it impossible for the Community to continue to function. In the event of the Community being obliged to disband, the house and lands of Posbury St Francis must be sold for the benefit of any Sisters who are in Life Vows.

If the Sisters should be able to set up a Chapel in the place to which they go, they must be allowed to take what they need of Chapel and Altar vessels and furnishings with them, otherwise the sacred vessels, vestments, etc. should be given by the Sisters to a poor Church or mission at their discretion.

This Constitution takes effect from January 1st, 1957, and may be subject to revision and addition by the Chapter, if a necessity has arisen, at the end of seven years. Any changes must be confirmed by a second meeting of the Chapter and with the consent of the Visitor.

Index of People, Places and Religious Communities

Andrew, Fr   6–11, 16, 58, 70
Andrews, R., Fr   43, 88, 114–15, 116
Assisi   vii, 58–60, 121, 145, 150, 165

Barbour, J.   37
Batten, M.   97
Baybrook Road, Hastings   1
Bedford, A., Duchess of   10
Bee, D. *see* Sister Clare   73, 74
Benson, M.   114, 178, *see also* Sister Bride
Betjeman, J.   41, 42, 43, 46
Beveridge, L.   152
Birmingham   65, 84, 167
Blisland   38, 41–6, 48, 57, 145, 147
Bolitho, T.B.   31, 37
Boston, Massachusetts, USA   10, 12, 16, 22, 36, 62
Boxall, M.   vii, 147
Bridgettine Order, South Brent   122, 135
Browne, Fr   57, 61–2, 65–67
Buckley, G., Dr   75, 108

Cape Cod   15–16,
Cary, L., Fr   36
Chapman, C.   vii, viii, xiv, 154, 158, 165
Chelsea 6–7
Christ Church, Folkestone   1
Christ Church, St. Leonards   6
Clarabut, E., Fr   41–2
Clarke Hall, W., Sir   23, 30
Clewer   135
Community of Mary the Virgin, Wantage   137

Community of St John the Divine, Plaistow   6
Community of St Mary, Kenosha, Wisconsin   15–16
Community of St Wilfrid, Exeter   98
Community of the Compassion of Jesus at West Ogwell   162
Community of the Epiphany, St Agnes   61, 67
Community of the Holy Cross, Haywards Heath   78
Community of the Resurrection, Mirfield   61, 65
Cope, M. *see* Sister Mary
Costin, A.   1
Costin, G.   xii, 1, 171, 177, *see also* Mother Teresa and Sister Teresa
Costin, T.   1
Cowes   86, 107, 110
Cowick Street, Exeter   122, 129
Coysh, D.   76, 177, *see also* Sister Bernadine
Crediton   93, 95, 97, 98, 99, 100, 107, 108, 109, 143, 155, 158, 160, 165, 166, 168
Creedy Park   117–18
Curzon, C., Bishop   vi, 75, 77, 81, 97, 104, 111, 117, 127,

Daunt, Mr and Mrs   96
Davison, E.   152
Davison, R. G., Fr   146, 152, 163, 164
Dawson, E.   3
Devonport   107
Dickens, Miss   30, 31

188

INDEX

Duxhurst, Surrey   8–10, 21, 24, 96

Emma (Walkes' maid)   34, 38, 41, 43–45, 47, 49, 51, 52, 74, 147
Exeter   93, 95–104, 106–7, 111, 113, 117, 121, 122, 127, 128, 131, 135, 137, 144–6, 148, 151, 152, 155, 156–7, 160, 162, 163, 165, 166, 169, 175
Exeter College, Oxford   128, 134, 164
Exeter University   152
Extern Brother James   167

Fairby Grange   23–5, 29, 30
Fennell, E.   78, 79, see also Sister Christina
Ferguson-Davie, P. Revd Sir   117, 153
Fetlar   150, 161
Folkestone   1
Fletcher, M.   74
Francis, St, of Assisi   31, 58–60, 108, 123, 129, 130, 142, 144, 171, 180, 184
Franciscan Servants of Jesus and Mary (FSJM)   vi–viii, ix, x, xiii, xiv, 56, 66, 74, 84, 85, 86, 88, 89, 93, 96, 100, 101–2, 104–10, 117, 120–6, 127–41, 142, 145, 147, 149–58, 159–69, 170–72, 173, 174, 177–9, 180–7
Frere. W., Bishop   61, 62, 64, 65
Fulham   5

Gault, C., Fr   xv, 137, 138, 140, 145–6, 153
Gendall, Fr   62
Gilbert, Fr   64
Gofton Salmon, R. Fr   74, 90
Gretna Green   18, 20

Hardy, Mrs   12–15
Hastings   3, 6, 35
Hermitage of Campello   59
Hillier, G.   84
Hinton Martell   69, 70, 85
Hippisley Tuckfield, R. Sir   95
Holy Trinity, Paisley   44, 156
Hooper, J. Fr   xv, 117, 123, 127, 129, 137, 145

Howe, J. Canon   134, 164
Hunkin, J. Bishop   121
Huddleston, T. Bishop   128

Ignatius, Fr   35
Inskip, D.,   86, 109, 178, see also Mother Hilary and Sister Hilary
Iona   53, 130, 149–50

Jacobs, W.   123
Jenkins, A.   147
Jenkinson, C.   179, see also Sister Faith

Kansas City, USA   12–17, 19–20
Kemp, E. Canon   164
Kemper Hall, Kenosha, USA   15, 17
Knight, L.   28

Langdon, C. G. Fr   71–77, 79–81
Larks of St Francis   60, 101, 121, 150
Lee, P. Fr   166–8
Ley, Dom Benedict   88
Llanthony Abbey   35, 40

Meeth   107, 121
Mercer, E., Bishop   137, 144, 156, 175
Merrymeet   137, 146, 153, 163, 166
Millington, P.   130, 179, see also Sister Agnes
Mortimer, Mrs   137
Mortimer, R., Bishop   117, 137
Mother Etheldred   62
Mother Hilary   vii, viii, ix, xiii, xv, 3, 133, 135, 137, 138, 140–1, 143, 146, 147, 149, 150–2, 153–8, see also Inskip, D. and Sister Hilary
Mother Ivy   9, 10, 16, 22, 36, 37, 44, 47, 54, 81, 82, 110–11
Mother Millicent   65
Mother Teresa   6–7, x, xii–xiii, 3, 21, 22, 43–6, 47–55, 56–67, 69–81, 82–90, 93–100, 101–112, 114–26, 127–41, 142–8, 149–69, 170–2, 173–6, 177, see also Costin, G.

Natusch, S.   119, 123

Oakley Crescent, London   vi, 72, 75, 98
O'Brien, Fr   127
Ocker Hill   134
Order of St Anne, Boston   xii, 10, 12, 21, 62
Oxford   vi, 7, 19–20, 128, 129, 134, 164

Paignton   136
Paisley   ix, xii, 44–5, 47–55, 61, 64, 65, 70, 74, 80, 84, 89, 114–16, 145, 147, 156, 16
Parsons, W.   3, 70
Partridge, F.   83
Pearce, M.   44, 177, *see also* Sister Margaret
Pizey, E., Fr   129, 137
Plympton St Maurice   156, 161
Poole, D.   85
Porta   105
Porthcurno   xv, 130, 152, 168, 172
Posbury   vi–viii, ix–xi, xii–xiii, xiv–xv, 93–100, 101–12, 114–26, 127–41, 144–6, 149–58, 159–69, 170–2, 173–6
Posbury Clump   vi, viii, 107–8, 121, 124
Posbury St Francis Trust   x, xiv, 172, 173
Powell, C., Fr   12–13, 22, 36
Priestcott, Posbury   95, 99, 122, 128, 134, 146, 164, 172, *see also* St Mary of the Angels

Richards, Francis   97
Richards, J   146
Richards, J. Bishop   155, 160, 173
Roberts, J.   xv, 128, 152, 168
Robertson, A., Fr   101
Robinson, M.   85
Rowden family   5
Rowe, A., Fr   163, 166
Rowse, A.L.   41
Royal Sea Bathing Hospital, Margate   7
Royal Surrey County Hospital   7

Salter, A., Dr   23
Salter, J. *see* Sister Giovanna   136, 179
Secombe, H., Sir   viii, 155
Sedgley   134

Sharpe, T., Fr   123
Shaw, E.   84, 115, 178, *see also* Sister Elizabeth
Shaw, M., Bishop   ix–xi, xiv, 132, 156, 166, 168
Sheppard, D., Bishop   87
Society of the Precious Blood, Burnham Abbey   65, 68
Sister Agnes   vii, xiv, 79, 131, 133, 135, 136, 143, 149–52, 161, 173–6, 179, *see also* Millington, P.
Sister Bernadine   vi, vii, 76–7, 78, 80, 85, 89, 99, 100, 102, 106, 107, 110, 111, 115, 132, 135, 136, 142, 177, *see also* Coysh, D.
Sister Bride   vii, viii, 114–18, 132, 137, 143, 156, 159, 161, 165, 178, *see also* Benson, M.
Sister Christina   79, *see also* Fennell, E.
Sister Clare   74, 78–9, 85, 88–9, 98, 110–11, 114, *see* Bee, D.
Sister Columba   149
Sister Elizabeth   vii, viii, xiii, xiv, 30, 84, 115–16, 132, 142, 145, 151, 156, 166, 175, 178, *see* Shaw, E. L.
Sister Faith   vii, 80, 85, 89, 99, 102, 103, 108, 110, 132, 138, 143, 145, 152, 155, 156, 159, 161, 176, 179, *see also* Jenkinson, C.
Sister Giovanna   vii, viii, xiv, 136, 140, 143, 144, 151, 153, 154, 155, 156, 159, 162, 164, 166–9, 179, *see also* Salter, J.
Sister Hilary   vii, 109, 110, 115, 116, 120–1, 132, 178, *see also* Mother Hilary and Inskip, D.
Sister Margaret   vi, 62, 69, 71, 73, 74, 76, 77, 78–79, 81, 82, 84, 87, 89, 96–8, 106–8, 110, 114–15, 116, 124, 125, 127, 135, 140, 142–5, 146, 148, 149, 156, 167, 170, 174, 176, 177, *see also* Pearce, M.
Sister Mary   vii, viii, 114–15, 116, 118, 119, 124, 130, 132–3, 135, 136, 141, 143, 149, 150, 151, 152, 153–5, 156–8, 159–60, 162, 171, 174, 175, 178, *see also* Cope, M.

INDEX

Sister Rosanna   8, 54, 81, 82, 110
Sister Teresa   xii, 22, *see also* Costin, G. and Mother Teresa
Sister Vi   152, 163, 167
Somerset, H. Lady   8, 11
Sorella Maria   60–1,
Sorella Jacopa   60
St Agnes, Cornwall   56–7, 61–6
St Blazey   62–4, 68
St Clement's, London   74, 77, 81, 87
St Gabriel, Plymouth   155
St Hilary, Cornwall   23, 26, 28–40, 41, 43, 45, 47–8, 53, 56–7, 89, 101, 121, 146, 164,
St Leonards-on-Sea   5, 57
St Luke's College   95, 103
St Luke's Chapel, Posbury   95, 97, 99, 108, 109, 119, 163, 169
St Mary of the Angles, Posbury   8, 123, 135, 142, 146, *see also* Priestcott
St Mewan   64
St Matthew's, City Road   71, 72, 81
St Philip, Plaistow   6
St Protus and St Hyacinth, Blisland   41
St Stephen's House, Oxford   164
St Stephen-in-Brannel   64
Surtees, W., Bishop   100

Tate, J., Fr   137
Taylor, D., Fr   69–71, 80
Terry, R.   76
Thurmer, J., Canon   157, 161, 175
Tindle, Chief Inspector   21
Tredinnick, M.   85

Underhill, E.   22, 59, 67, 82, 87, 90

Walke, B., Fr   vi, xii, 23–6, 28–40, 41, 49, 51, 52, 73, 80, 89, 121, 146, 147, 164
Walke, A.   vi, 30, 32
Well Meadow, Paisley   47, 48
Whan Cross   87
Whitwell   vi, 54, 55, 81–2, 82–90, 98
Wilson, L. R., Canon   xiv, 3, 146
Winnington-Ingram, A., Bishop   74
Woodrow, M.   74, 153

Figure 6: The main house at Posbury with its thatch prior to the reroofing in slate in 1963. In front of the chapel to the left is Sister Mary's greenhouse and her well-established herbaceous border can be seen on the right.

Figure 7: The chapel at Posbury converted from a former stable block. The door leads into the main body of the chapel, the half dormer window lights the priest's bedroom above the sacristy and to its right lies the priest's sitting room.

Figure 8: Photograph marking the clothing of Sister Mary and Sister Bride on 26 April 1946. Sister Mary, to the left of Mother Teresa and Sister Bride to her right wear the round collar of a novice. Seated on the ground are Sister Bernadine and Sister Hilary to the right.

Figure 9: Sister Hilary, departing in some style for her pilgrimage to Assisi in 1951, being bid farewell by Sister Mary.

Figure 10: Sister Agnes outside the front door at Posbury on the day she made her life vows, 1 July 1969.

Figure 11: Mother Hilary and Sister Faith on the front lawn at Posbury with their dog Leo in the 1970s. On the hillside in the distance is Posbury Clump bought by the sisters to save the trees from being felled.

Figure 12: Group photo of the sisters outside the backdoor at Posbury in the late 1980s. From left to right Sister Bride, Sister Elizabeth, Mother Hilary, Sister Mary, Sister Faith and Sister Giovanna—seated with their dog Max. Sisters Bride, Mary and Giovanna are wearing their gardening clothes.

Figure 13: Sister Mary seated on her tractor with Mother Hilary holding Max, and Sister Giovanna. They are accompanied by Extern Sister Molly Boxall, who lived nearby and nursed Mother Teresa while she was dying. Photo © Chris Chapman.

Figure 14: Mother Hilary seated in the kitchen at Posbury with from left to right Sisters Bride, Elizabeth and Mary. Behind them was the habitually running aga which made the room one of the most welcoming in the house. The jug on the table and poster on the wall are souvenirs from their pilgrimages to Assisi. Photo © Chris Chapman.

Figure 15: The garden altar rescued from the graveyard at St Hilary in 1953 with a surround built by the sisters from blocks of red sandstone brought from Posbury Clump. The reproduction della Robbia plaque was brought back from a pilgrimage to Italy.

Figure 16: Mother Hilary poses with the broadcaster
Sir Harry Secombe, Sister Mary and Sister Giovanna
after he visited the FSJM in the 1980s.

Figure 17: Service of Benediction at the garden altar at the conclusion
of an Open Day - the juxtaposition of High Anglican practice,
natural setting and family atmosphere typical of the FSJM.

Figure 18: Photograph of Sister Giovanna and Mother Hilary from the exhibition *A Positive View of the Third Age.* Photo © Chris Chapman.

EU GPSR Authorized Representative:

LOGOS EUROPE, 9 rue Nicolas Poussin, 17000 La Rochelle, France

contact@logoseurope.eu